Artfully Transforming

BOTTLES & PLATES

75 Elegant Projects to Upcycle
Glass and Porcelain

Petra Knoblauch · Ina Mielkau

SCHIFFER
CRAFT

4880 Lower Valley Road • Atglen, PA 19310

OTHER SCHIFFER BOOKS ON RELATED SUBJECTS:

Vintage Cardboard Crafting: Handmaking 15 Embellished Containers, Anne Lardy, ISBN 978-0-7643-5965-1

Upcycling Books: Decorative Objects, Julia Rubio, ISBN 978-0-7643-5875-3

Weaving: The Art of Sustainable Textile Creation, Maria Sigma, ISBN 978-0-7643-6038-1

Translated from the German by Catherine Venner.

Originally published as *Resteliebe Glas* by Ina Mielkau and *Resteliebe Porzellan* by Petra Knoblauch, both © 2021 Christophorus Verlag / Christian Verlag GmbH, Munich.

Library of Congress Control Number: 2022944317

Designed by Ina Mielkau
Cover design by Ashley Millhouse
Type set in Mrs. Eaves/Avenir Next
Pages 4–5, 8–129:
Photos and illustrations: Ina Mielkau
Project management: Svenja Wiglinghaus

Pages 3, 6–7, 130–247:
Photos and illustrations: Frank Moldenhauer
Project management: Svenja Wiglinghaus

ISBN: 978-0-7643-6619-2
Printed in China

Published by Schiffer Publishing, Ltd.
4880 Lower Valley Road
Atglen, PA 19310
Phone: (610) 593–1777; Fax: (610) 593–2002
Email: Info@schifferbooks.com
Web: www.schifferbooks.com

For our complete selection of fine books on this and related subjects, please visit our website at www.schifferbooks.com. You may also write for a free catalog.

Schiffer Publishing's titles are available at special discounts for bulk purchases for sales promotions or premiums. Special editions, including personalized covers, corporate imprints, and excerpts, can be created in large quantities for special needs. For more information, contact the publisher.

We are always looking for people to write books on new and related subjects. If you have an idea for a book, please contact us at proposals@schifferbooks.com.

CONTENTS

Glass | by Ina Mielkau

Porcelain | by Petra Knoblauch

GLASS

INA MIELKAU

Introduction

It isn't hard to cut glass. It just takes a little patience, since it doesn't always work on the first try and there may be a couple of broken bottles to start off with. But don't let that discourage you: often bottles have already been recycled and so the strength of the glass varies very widely, which means that if it can't be evenly cut, it's due to the glass itself.

One or two bottles broke as I worked on the projects for this book. So it's worthwhile cultivating a small collection of bottles just in case. Friends and acquaintances have always been happy to provide me with empty bottles . . . after all, I'm actually saving them a trip to the recycling center.

It's important to follow safety measures so that you do not injure yourself. When working, always wear safety glasses and, when possible, protective gloves too, no matter what method you're using to cut the bottle. Always remove the stopper or cork from the bottle beforehand. You should always have sandpaper handy so that you can immediately smooth the edges of the glass.

All the bottle projects in this book have been made using a glass cutter that I bought especially for my craft work. This tool has proven to be the best for cutting, and it significantly increases the likelihood of a good result. Glass cutters can be bought cheaply on the internet. So if you intend to work on glass bottles frequently, it's a wise purchase.

You can also find instructions online to make your own glass cutter. The majority of these instructions were somewhat too complicated for me, except for one design, which I teach you to make here. Although you can't continuously adjust its cutting height, the cutting result is very good.

Enjoy making with bottles!

What's Waste Glass?

Waste glass is glass that has been used as "packaging" and is collected for recycling afterward.

After processing, the waste glass arrives as a usable raw material at a glass factory and is recycled. It is primarily used for the production of more glass packaging. In comparison to producing new glass, it saves a large amount of energy and raw materials.

Tips and Tricks

LABELS

Bottle labels provide important information for the consumer. However, if you want to reuse the bottles, you have to pull off the individual scraps of paper, which can be a laborious task! It requires a lot of patience and strong nerves . . .

. . . or a bit of imagination. Here are my tips: For these projects, I generally placed the bottles in a bucket of water the day before to allow the labels to soften. As a rule, at least one layer of the paper could be peeled off at that point. For the remainder, I used a stainless-steel scouring pad from the cleaning cupboard. Instead of pulling off the bits of paper with your fingers, you simply rub over the bottle with the scourer. It works really well!

Grease is also a good alternative. Apply cooking oil or margarine with a cloth and allow it to sink in. It reduces the adhesiveness of the label so that it can be pulled away with your fingers. You may have to repeat this process a few times.

A hairdryer is rather unsuitable for large bottle labels, and it's not very energy-saving. Turpentine and nail polish remover are also unnecessary. It's better to soak the labels in water.

CORKS

Corks are wonderful as lids or stoppers for jars you make from bottles. However, always remember to measure the diameter of the jars.

Natural corks are very decorative but also rather expensive. I use the significantly cheaper agglomerated cork, which is made from byproducts of natural-cork production. The cork granules are pressed into shape using an adhesive.

Agglomerated cork is impermeable and it's easier to drill into than natural cork; for instance, if you need to attach a cord or insert a straw.

Cutting Bottles

THE BASIC PRINCIPLE

The principle for cutting bottles is similar for each method. A spot on the bottle is "weakened" and then "stressed" by changing its temperature until it breaks in the desired place.

To do this, you scratch around the desired breaking point. You can use a glass cutter. Simple glass cutters can be purchased at a hardware store for a few dollars. But freehand glass cutting is not really the best choice here. A special glass cutter for bottles, which can be bought on the internet, is better suited.

If you have neither a glass cutter nor a special bottle cutter, then you could try the simple method using a cotton string and denatured alcohol, nail polish remover, or lighter fuel. However, the result isn't always successful.

It's important to observe a few safety measures. Glass has sharp edges, and when it breaks, small shards fly off. So always wear protective gloves and safety glasses when working.

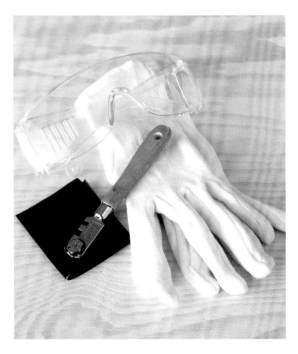

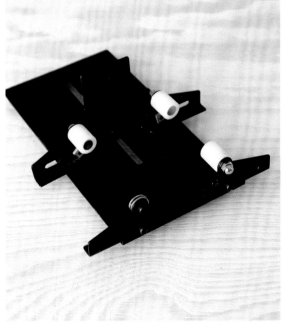

METHOD 1. CUTTING WITHOUT A GLASS CUTTER.
YOU WILL NEED COTTON STRING, DENATURED ALCOHOL (ALTERNATIVELY LIGHTER
FUEL OR NAIL POLISH REMOVER), AND A PAN OR BUCKET OF ICE-COLD WATER.

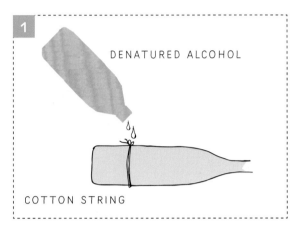

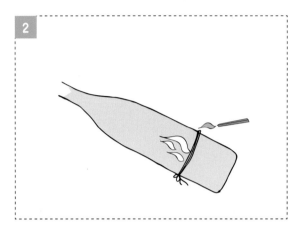

1. First, soak the cotton string in denatured alcohol. Then wrap it securely around the desired breaking point on the bottle and tie in place. If the string is very thin, then you can wrap it around the bottle two or three times. Cut off the ends.

2. Touch a flame to the string until it burns. Then wait for the string to burn away. While the string is burning, turn the bottle so that the heat is evenly distributed.

3. When the string has burned away, dunk the bottle in the bucket or pan of cold water. Now the bottle should break at the desired breaking point. If not, repeat the process and consider using a thicker string.

4. Smooth the edges, using very fine sandpaper.

METHOD 2. CUTTING WITH A BOTTLE CUTTER OR GLASS CUTTER.
YOU'LL NEED A BOTTLE CUTTER (OR A GLASS CUTTER) AS WELL AS HOT AND
COLD WATER.

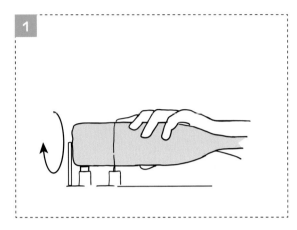

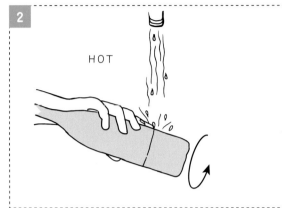

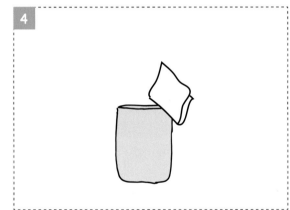

1. Using the bottle cutter, cleanly scratch a full circle around the bottle.

If you don't have a special bottle cutter, you can wrap tape around the bottle to mark it. Then cut along the tape edge with the glass cutter.

2. Pour boiling water evenly over the scratch. While you're pouring, turn the bottle.

Alternatively, you can rotate the scratched line over a flame to heat it.

3. Next, pour ice-cold water over the scratch. While you're pouring, turn the bottle.

In the ideal scenario, part of the bottle will break off with a soft crack. If not, repeat the process with hot and cold water.

4. Then smooth the edges with very fine sandpaper.

THE BEST WAY TO CUT A BOTTLE IS WITH A SPECIAL BOTTLE CUTTER. THE EDGES ARE SMOOTHER AND IT'S SAFER THAN USING AN OPEN FLAME.

How to Construct a Bottle Cutter

MATERIALS:
APPROX. 6.5' OF SQUARE WOODEN BATTENS
(0.75" × 0.75"), WOODEN BOARD (APPROX.
8" × 14"), PENCIL, RULER, MITER BOX, SAW,
WOOD GLUE, SCREW CLAMP, GLASS CUTTER

IF YOU DON'T WANT TO BUY A BOTTLE CUTTER, YOU CAN EASILY MAKE ONE YOURSELF. THE INSTRUCTIONS FOUND ON THE INTERNET CAN BE VERY COMPLICATED. THIS IS A METHOD THAT'S SIMPLE AND PRACTICAL, AND, OF COURSE, IT WORKS.

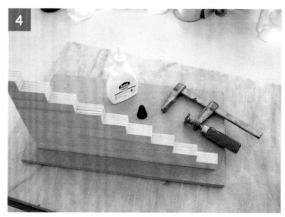

1. Collect your materials to make the bottle cutter.

2. First cut the square battens to different lengths. I used the following measurements: 13, 12, 10, 8.5, 7, 5.5, 4, 2, and 0.75 in.

3. Stick the individual battens to each other using the wood glue and then leave them to dry for half a day. This top part should look like a small staircase.

4. Once dried, stick the "staircase" to the cut-to-size board. Position it so you leave some space to the left, right, and front. The glue should also be allowed to dry well at this stage.

Later, you can attach the board to a table edge using a clamp. Also use a clamp to attach the simple glass cutter to one of the steps. When doing so, ensure that the small wheel on the glass cutter is far enough forward so that it firmly touches the glass (see the next page).

THE BOTTLES ARE PRESSED DIRECTLY ONTO THE GLASS CUTTER FROM BEHIND AND TURNED EVENLY. WHILE TURNING THE BOTTLE, BE SURE THAT ITS BOTTOM IS ALWAYS FIRMLY PLACED ON THE BOARD. IT'S BEST TO MAINTAIN AN EVEN PRESSURE THROUGHOUT ONE TURN OF THE BOTTLE.

The Lower Part
of the Bottle

THE BOTTOM OF EVERY BOTTLE IS DIFFERENT. MOST OF THEM ARE VERY CONCAVE, AND THERE ARE MANY THEORIES ABOUT THE REASON. DOES IT MAKE IT EASIER FOR WAITERS TO POUR GLASSES IN RESTAURANTS? IS IT A TRICK BY THE BEVERAGE INDUSTRY TO GIVE THE IMPRESSION OF MORE CONTENT? DOES IT HAVE SOMETHING TO DO WITH THE PRODUCTION OF THE BOTTLES?

THE REASON IS ACTUALLY THE PRESSURE THAT'S TRYING TO ESCAPE, IN PARTICULAR IN THE CASE OF SPARKLING WINE OR CHAMPAGNE. THE WEAK POINTS OF A BOTTLE ARE THE BOTTLENECK AND BOTTOM. AT THE TOP, THE CORK SEALS THE CONTAINER. THAT LEAVES THE BOTTOM OF THE BOTTLE, WHERE THE CURVE WORKS AGAINST THE PRESSURE AND EVENLY DISTRIBUTES IT TO THE BOTTLE SIDES.

Sugar Body Scrub

INGREDIENTS:
SUGAR, LEMON OR LIME (OR LAVENDER),
SOAP COLORING, OLIVE OIL
MATERIALS:
BOTTOM OF A BOTTLE, CORK, BOWL,
SPOON, ZESTER, LABEL

THIS CITRUS OR LAVENDER BODY SCRUB, WHICH IS NATURALLY HOMEMADE AND PACKED PRETTILY IN A JAR WITH A CORK AND LABEL, IS A GREAT PRESENT FOR YOUR BEST FRIEND OR A LOVELY TREAT FOR YOURSELF.

1. Collect your supplies for the body scrub.

2. Pour the sugar into the decorative jar to establish how much it can hold. Then pour the sugar into a bowl. Mix in some olive oil but ensure that the mixture doesn't become too smooth.

3. Then mix in the juice of half a lemon or half a lime.

If you like, add one or two drops of yellow soap coloring to give the scrub a more intense color.

4. Then mix in the grated zest of the lemon or lime.

Now that the body scrub has been prepared, pour it into the clean jar and seal with a cork.

A beautifully designed label is an additional loving touch.

You can find the label templates on page 128.

TO MAKE THE LAVENDER BODY SCRUB, USE COCONUT OIL INSTEAD OF OLIVE OIL SO THAT THE SUGAR DOESN'T TURN YELLOW. THEN ALL YOU NEED TO DO IS ADD A FEW SCENT-ED LAVENDER FLOWERS AND SOME LAVENDER OIL.

LAVENDER
BODYSCRUB

HANDMADE WITH
SUGAR & LOVE

Absolute Transparency

MATERIALS:
LOWER PART OF BOTTLE, TRANSPARENT
STICKER, CORK STOPPER

TRANSPARENT STICKERS ALLOW THE CONTENT OF JARS TO BE EASILY VISIBLE AND CAN BE QUICKLY AFFIXED WITHOUT MUCH FUSS. ALL YOU NEED IS A TRANSPARENT STICKER AND A CORK STOPPER, AND THE STORAGE JAR IS COMPLETE. THEY MAKE LOVELY GIFTS FOR GOOD FRIENDS, FILLED WITH SOMETHING WONDERFUL OF COURSE!

1. Affix the chosen transparent sticker to the prepared jars. Then fill up the jar with some tasty goodies. Use a stopper made of natural or agglomerated cork as the lid.

2. To present as a gift, package the jar in a small wooden box with wood shavings. A bonus: the wool shavings provide extra padding during transportation.

WHETHER ON YOUR DESK OR IN THE BATHROOM, THE LOWER PARTS OF BOTTLES ARE PERFECT FOR STORING THINGS. YOU CAN DECORATE A SMALL HANDMADE JAR WITH TAPE OR A STICKY LABEL AND USE CORK TO CLOSE IT.

PADS

TO QUICKLY DECORATE JARS MADE FROM THE LOWER PARTS OF BOTTLES, SIMPLY PRINT A MOTIF ON TRANS-LUCENT PAPER, CUT IT OUT, AND STICK IT TO THE JAR. IT MAKES A LOVELY CANDLEHOLDER OR PEN HOLDER.

Cookies for You!

MATERIALS:
AIR-DRYING MODELING CLAY, ROLLING PIN,
KNIFE OR CUTTER, RULER, STAMP, SKEWER
OR CHOPSTICK, LOWER PART OF A BOTTLE,
SANDPAPER, TWINE

WHO SAID THAT LABELS HAVE TO BE MADE OF PAPER? WHAT ABOUT USING A LABEL MADE OF MODELING CLAY TO DECORATE A GIFT JAR? NATURALLY, YOU CAN ALSO USE THESE LABELS ON YOUR OWN JARS TO STORE SWEET TREATS.

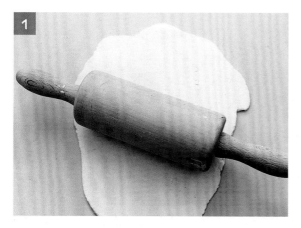

1. Roll out the air-drying modeling clay to a thickness of 3 to 4 mm.

2. Use the cutter to cut the clay into rectangles.

3. Press the letter stamps or pattern stamps into the still-soft clay and then use the skewer to bore holes for the twine.

4. It's best to place the label on the jar to dry so that it takes on the correct curve.

5. Once it's dry, you can smooth out the label with sandpaper. Pull the twine through the holes and tie it around the jar.

TEA LIGHTS ARE ALWAYS A GOOD IDEA, WHETHER YOU ARE
INDOORS OR OUTDOORS. SO WHY NOT DRESS THE TEA LIGHT
HOLDER IN A GRASS SKIRT? ATTACH THE CUT STRIPS TO
SOME TWINE AND THEN TIE IT AROUND THE HOLDER.

Tea Lights

SMALL FLOATING TEA LIGHT HOLDERS ARE WONDERFUL. ALL
YOU NEED TO DO IS FILL THE JAR WITH WATER AND PLACE
THE HOLDER AND TEA LIGHT ON TOP! OR SIMPLY USE A
PRETTY FLOATING CANDLE.

Scratching the
Surface

MATERIALS:
LOWER PART OF A BOTTLE, TEMPLATE
(PAGE 129), ADHESIVE, CLOTH, ENGRAVING
DEVICE (E.G., DREMEL), SAFETY GLASSES,
PROTECTIVE MASK

ENGRAVING SOUNDS MORE COMPLICATED THAT IT ACTUALLY IS; ALL YOU NEED IS THE NECESSARY TOOLS. IT WOULD BE A REAL SHAME TO HAVE NEVER GIVEN IT A TRY. YOU JUST NEED A LITTLE COURAGE IF THIS IS NEW TO YOU, AND NOTHING CAN REALLY GO WRONG.

1. For engraving, you need a multifunction device that you can also engrave with. It should be small and easy to handle. Make sure it has the attachments you need.

First cut out a template for the engraving and fix it inside the jar, using glue. For your first attempt, use a less complicated pattern. The template used for this project can be found on page 129.

2. Place the jar on a soft cloth so that it doesn't slide around as you work. Using a small rest (such as a book) for your hand is also a good idea.

Wear safety glasses and, if necessary, a protective mask. Then start to engrave (follow the instructions for the device). It works best to outline the shapes first and then to fill them in.

Now and then, use a cloth to wipe away the fine dust that's created when engraving.

Good Things Come in Little Dishes

MATERIALS:
BOTTOMS OF TWO BOTTLES, WOODEN
BATTEN OFFCUTS, SAW, WOOD GLUE, CHALK
PAINT, BRUSH, PERMANENT MARKER,
(OPTIONAL) CORNER EMBELLISHMENTS

YUM . . . OLIVES! BUT AS YOU ENJOY THEM, WHAT SHOULD YOU DO WITH THE PITS? THEY DON'T LOOK VERY ATTRACTIVE ON THE EDGE OF THE PLATE. IT'S BETTER TO COLLECT THEM IN A SMALL DISH CRAFTED ESPECIALLY FOR THE PURPOSE! BOTTLES WITH A VERY DEEP BOTTOM INDENT ARE PERFECT FOR THIS.

1. If you want you can also make a small wooden tray tailored to the size of your dishes. It's easy: simply glue together the wooden battens that you've cut to size.

2. Once the glue has dried, you can paint the tray using chalk paint. Allow it to dry well.

3. If desired, you can decorate the corners.

4. To label the dishes, stick a template inside the glass and then go over it on the outside of the glass with a permanent marker.

If you don't have neat handwriting, you can of course just use a sticker.

Tattoo for You

MATERIALS:
JAR MADE FROM BROWN BOTTLE, CORK STOPPER, TEMPORARY TATTOOS IN GOLD AND SILVER, WATER, (OPTIONAL) SPONGE OR CLOTH

BROWN BOTTLES WITH TEMPORARY TATTOOS IN GOLD AND SILVER MAKE RATHER COOL STORAGE JARS. THE CONTENT IS PROTECTED BOTH FROM THE LIGHT AND FROM CURIOUS EYES. A LID MADE OF NATURAL CORK CLOSES IN WHATEVER YOU WANT TO STORE OR GIFT.

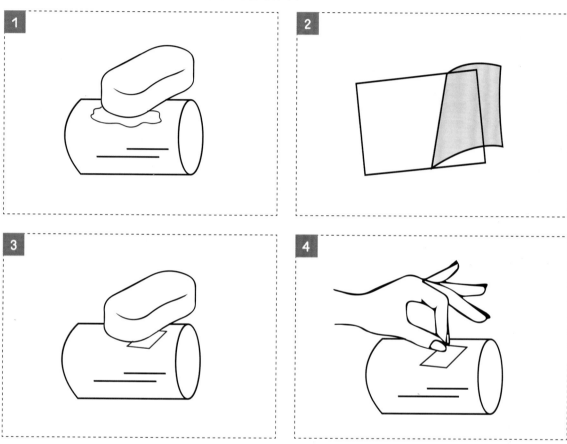

1. First, clean the jar well.

2. Remove the protective sheet from the tattoo.

3. Place the tattoo on the jar. Use a sponge or damp cloth to soak the paper for a moment. Be careful not to disturb the tattoo!

4. Carefully remove the paper and allow the tattoo to dry.

Most purchased temporary tattoos come with instructions that you can follow.

TEMPORARY TATTOOS ARE A QUICK AND SIMPLE OPTION
FOR DECORATING A JAR. SILVER AND GOLD LOOK BEST
ON DARK GLASS. THE TATTOO METHOD CAN BE USED TO
CREATE A TEA LIGHT HOLDER OUT OF THE BOTTOM OF A
BOTTLE.

Cocktail Hour

COCKTAIL HOUR WITH YOUR UNIQUE TOUCH! CUT BOTTLES
CAN ALSO BE USED AS DRINKING GLASSES. HOWEVER, THE
EDGES MUST BE REALLY WELL SMOOTHED, PREFERABLY
USING SPECIAL DIAMOND SANDPAPER.

Breakfast Is Ready!

MATERIALS:
BOTTOM OF A BOTTLE, LEATHER SCRAPS,
SCISSORS, LEATHER HOLE PUNCH, EYELET
PLIERS, EYELETS

SOME BOTTLES, MAINLY THE ONES FOR SPARKLING WINE OR CHAMPAGNE, HAVE AN EXTREMELY CONCAVE BOTTOM. THEY'RE JUST RIGHT FOR MAKING EGG CUPS JAZZED UP WITH A LEATHER STRIP! THESE ARE GUARANTEED TO BE AN EYE-CATCHER ON A DECKED-OUT BREAKFAST TABLE.

1. Use the scissors to cut the leather strip to a suitable length. The edges should overlap by about one-third of an inch. Use the leather punch to make two holes on each end of the length. Position the holes over each other and insert the eyelets.

2. Use the eyelet pliers to press the eyelets together.

3. Then place the leather band around the glass.

4. Place a boiled egg in the bottom. Breakfast is ready!

For Delicate Plants

MATERIALS:
LOWER PART OF A BOTTLE, CORK SHEET,
FELT-TIP PEN, CUTTER OR SCISSORS, A PLANT
OR CUTTING WITH DEVELOPING ROOTS

THIS PROJECT LETS YOU TO SEE WHAT IS NORMALLY CONCEALED. PLANTS'
LOWER PORTIONS CAN BE VERY INTERESTING TOO. THIS VASE ALLOWS YOU TO
WATCH BOTH ENDS OF THE PLANT GROW.

1. Use the jar as a template for the circle. Draw
the circle on a thin sheet of cork, about 3 mm
thick (or you could use foam rubber).

Cut out the circle. Remember to cut off a little
extra so that it fits snugly inside the glass. In the
center of your circle, cut out a smaller circle.

2. Fill the lower part of the bottle with water.
Push the plant through the hole in the cork and
then place the circle in the vase.

Later you can move the plant on to its next
home, but meanwhile, enjoy.

Super Models

MATERIALS:
LOWER PART OF A BOTTLE, AIR-DRYING
MODELING CLAY, PASTA MACHINE OR
ROLLING PIN, SANDPAPER, CLEAR VARNISH

FLOWERS GROWING ON THE SIDE OF THE ROAD OR IN MEADOWS ARE OFTEN SO ENCHANTING. AND WHAT COULD BE MORE SUITABLE FOR SUCH A POSY THAN AN UPCYCLED VASE LIKE THIS? IT'S MADE FROM A WHITE OR PALE-BLUE GLASS BOTTLE, SIMPLY DECORATED WITH A WHITE JACKET FORMED WITH AIR-DRYING CLAY.

1. Flatten the modeling clay using an old pasta machine. You can use a rolling pin, but it works better with a pasta machine because the clay comes out with an even thickness.

2. While rolling the clay, keep checking the length to ensure that the clay will wrap around the vase once. Press the overlapping edges together well and smooth them over. Also press the bottom edge under the vase into the curve.

3. Allow the modeling clay to dry completely. Then smooth out any unevenness using sand-paper. If desired, apply a layer of clear varnish.

Even with the varnish applied, you should still take care to avoid getting the clay wet.

Setting the Mood

MATERIALS:
BOTTOM OF A BOTTLE, MASKING TAPE, GOLD
SPRAY PAINT, LEFTOVER CANDLES OR WAX
PELLETS, A CONTAINER FOR MELTING WAX,
CANDLE WICKS, (OPTIONAL) TWEEZERS

IT'S A WELL-KNOWN FACT THAT YOU CAN NEVER HAVE ENOUGH CANDLES, WHETHER OUTSIDE ON THE PATIO AND IN THE YARD DURING THE SUMMER, OR INSIDE FOR COZY EVENINGS ON THE SOFA. SOMEHOW, THESE SMALL FLICKERING LIGHTS HAVE SUCH A CALMING EFFECT, DON'T YOU THINK?

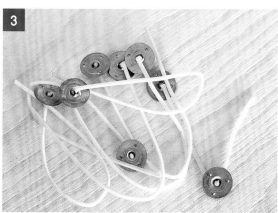

1. Fix masking tape around the prepared jars and spray the jars with spray paint. Once the paint has dried properly, remove the tape carefully to reveal the stripes.

2. Melt the leftover candles or wax pellets in an old pan.

3. Use the type of wick with a metal tab that enables you to position the wick.

4. Place the wick in the jar. The wick should be long enough that a piece extends far above the top of the jar. Since the majority of bottle bottoms are curved, you will have to hold the wick in place initially. Begin pouring in melted wax. Once there's enough wax in the jar, the wick can be held in place using tweezers. Fill the jar and cool.

When using a simple wick without a metal tab, tie the wick around a small wooden stick and hang the wick in the jar.

Winter Magic

FOR A LITTLE CHRISTMAS ATMOSPHERE OR SIMPLY AS A SOUVENIR OF YOUR LAST SKI TRIP, ALL YOU NEED IS A SMALL AMOUNT OF MOSS, A SCATTERING OF ARTIFICIAL SNOW, AND A COUPLE OF TINY TREES. AND VOILÀ—WINTER MAGIC!

The Upper Part
of the Bottle

BOTTLE BASICS: THE CONICAL TAPERED END OF A BOTTLE IS KNOWN AS THE BOTTLENECK. IT LEADS INTO A ROUND OPENING THAT SERVES AS THE SPOUT AND CAN BE SEALED.

TODAY, THE MAJORITY OF DRINKING AND STORAGE BOTTLES HAVE A SCREW TOP TO SEAL THEM. WHEN RECLOSING THE BOTTLE ISN'T NECESSARY, BEVERAGE BOTTLES SOMETIMES HAVE BOTTLE CAPS. NOWADAYS, WE SEE CORKS ONLY ON WINE BOTTLES, ALTHOUGH THE SCREW TOP IS POPULAR FOR THEM AS WELL.

Cool Lanterns

MATERIALS:
UPPER PART OF A BOTTLE, DECO-
RATION, COASTER, TEA LIGHTS

JUST THE RIGHT THING FOR WHEN THERE'S SOME WIND AND YOU DON'T WANT TO GO WITHOUT CANDLELIGHT OUTSIDE. THE UPPER PARTS OF THE BOTTLE CAN BE DECORATED IN YOUR STYLE AND PLACED ON A SMALL COASTER.

1. One decorating option is to wind twine around the bottleneck. Putting twine there is also practical since it allows you to safely touch the bottle after use when it's hot from the candle's flame.

2. Using modeling clay—we used a cement color—make small tags and tie them to the bottles. Or you could make small chains with wooden beads and hang them around the bottleneck.

3. You can make the coasters out of wood scraps or you can use small bowls.

There should be enough room for a large tea light or a small pillar candle.

Glimmers of Light

MATERIALS FOR 1 LAMP:
UPPER PART OF A BOTTLE, SMALL JAR
WITH A LIP, WIRE, PLIERS, LINK CHAIN,
2 KEY RINGS

TEA LIGHTS DON'T HAVE TO SIT AROUND; THEY CAN ALSO BE HUNG UP. THEY'RE PARTICULARLY PRETTY WHEN HANGING IN THE GARDEN OR OUT ON THE BALCONY. WITH THESE LANTERNS, IF THE BOTTLES MOVE SLIGHTLY IN THE WIND, IT DOESN'T BLOW OUT THE TEA LIGHTS.

1. Cut the chain to the desired length and attach one of the key rings to one end.

2. Thread two short pieces of chain on a piece of wire that loosely goes around the small jar twice. The length of the chain is dependent on the height of the jar. Wind the wire around the jar and weave in the ends.

3. Attach the ends of the short chains to the key ring that is attached to the long link chain.

4. Now take the free end of the chain and thread the whole chain from below through the bottle and out the top. Then attach the other key ring to the top of the chain. This ring prevents the chain from falling back into the bottle and also can be used for hanging up the finished lamp.

LANTERNS ON A STICK? WHY NOT? TAKE A WOODEN STAKE OR ROD, A COPPER PIPE COLLAR FROM THE HARDWARE STORE, AND A TUNA FISH CAN. SCREW EVERYTHING TOGETHER AND PAINT THE UPPER PART. AND THERE YOU HAVE IT—AN ENCHANTED GARDEN.

THERE'S ALSO A SIMPLER VERSION: JUST PLACE THE LANTERN OVER A CANDLE. IT LOOKS PRETTY ON STEPS.

Let There Be Light!

MATERIALS:
UPPER PART OF BOTTLE, LAMP HOLDER
KIT, SCREWDRIVER, CORK, DRILL

WHY NOT GIVE LAMP DESIGN A TRY? IT'S REALLY EASY. THE HOLDER KITS FOR THE LAMP CAN BE FOUND IN HARDWARE STORES OR ELECTRICAL-SUPPLY SHOPS. YOU NEED TO EITHER DRINK THE BOTTLES EMPTY YOURSELF OR HAVE A FRIEND DO IT FOR YOU.

1. It's easiest to buy a ready-made lamp holder kit from the hardware store, and it may even have a switch and plug attached. The advantage is that they usually include instructions.

It's important to pay attention to the correct sequence of steps for your lamp holder style. In this case, you first insert the cord through the drilled cork and then thread the cord into the bottle from the top.

2. Only then, screw the holder together according to the instructions. If you're unsure, seek help from an electrician.

Continued on the next page

3. Sometimes the kits also include a small threaded rod, through which you can feed the cord. Once everything is in the correct position, you can screw in a suitable lightbulb.

4. Carefully pull the cord upward and press the cork firmly into the bottle.

For the sake of safety, use superglue or a glue gun to firmly stick the cork to the edge of the glass so that it doesn't slip out of the bottle as the lamp is hanging. You can still adjust the cord in the drilled hole. However, it should sit very tight.

Now, you can hang the bottle on a hook, with a loop knot.

YOU CAN ALSO DECORATE OR PAINT
THE LAMPS. WITH THAT DESIGNER
TOUCH, THE LAMP LOOKS GREAT ON A
BEDSIDE TABLE.

Round Peg, Square Hole?

MATERIALS:
UPPER PART OF A BOTTLE, WOOD BLOCK, DRILL WITH FORSTNER BIT, STRING, (OPTIONAL) SAW

LION

SAFETY MATCHES

WHAT CAN YOU DO WITH ALL THE UPPER HALVES THAT ARE LEFT OVER FROM MAKING JARS AND VASES? THE SIMPLEST SOLUTION IS TO MAKE CANDLEHOLDERS. IT'S SUPER-PRACTICAL BECAUSE CANDLES FIT PERFECTLY IN THE TAPERED BOTTLENECK.

1. For the bottle holder, ask for a suitable block of wood to be cut off at the hardware store or lumberyard. It should have a minimum depth of 2 in. The blocks in this example are from an extremely old timber beam and are 4.25 by 4.2 in. and 2 in. thick.

Using a Forstner bit, drill a deep hole into the center of the block (be careful not to drill through it!). The diameter of the hole should correspond to the diameter of the bottleneck, preferably slightly larger. Then smooth all the sides of the block using sandpaper.

2. Insert the upper part of the bottle. If there's too much room in the hole for the bottle, fill the space using a thick piece of string. Wrap the string around the bottleneck and, using some-thing pointy (like a toothpick), push the string into the hole until the space has been filled.

Once everything is secure, you can insert a candle. Ta-dah!

Silver and Gold

WHEN PAINTED SILVER, THE UPPER PARTS OF BOTTLES ARE A PERFECT ALTERNATIVE ADVENT WREATH. AND A CANDLE DRIPPING ONTO A GOLDEN BOTTLENECK CAN ALSO LOOK VERY DECORATIVE.

Self-Watering Plants

MATERIALS:
UPPER AND LOWER PARTS OF A BOTTLE,
MESH SCREEN, COTTON STRING, SCISSORS,
PLANTS, COMPOST OR SOIL, WATER

IF YOU DON'T HAVE GREEN FINGERS, THIS PROJECT COULD BE A GREAT SOLUTION. WATERING PLANTS IS SO YESTERDAY! ... JUST ADD A LITTLE WATER TO THE LOWER PART NOW AND THEN, AND THE REST TAKES CARE OF ITSELF.

1. You'll need both parts of a cut bottle. The upper part should not be too long.

A small, undemanding plant, such as a succulent, is well suited for this project.

2. Cut two small pieces of the mesh screen, place them on top of each other, and cut a small hole in the center of them. Feed a couple of strands of the cotton string through the hole. The string should extend beyond the bottom of the bottleneck. Knot the string above the netting.

Continued on the next page

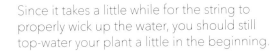

3. Carefully fill the upper part of the bottle with compost or soil and insert the small plant.

4. Half-fill the lower part of the bottle with water and position the upper part with the plant in it.

Since it takes a little while for the string to properly wick up the water, you should still top-water your plant a little in the beginning.

AFTER A WHILE, THE PLANT ROOTS MAY START TO
GROW DOWNWARD INTO THE BOTTLENECK. ALSO, A
LITTLE BIT OF SOIL MAY OCCASIONALLY SLIP DOWN
INTO THE JAR. SO RINSE OUT THE JAR EVERY ONCE
IN A WHILE AND GIVE THE PLANT FRESH WATER.

Colorful Vases

SOME BOTTLES ARE SO PRETTY THAT YOU
DON'T NEED TO GIVE THEM ANY FURTHER
DECORATION. THE INDIVIDUAL PARTS CAN BE
MIXED AND MATCHED OR KEPT TOGETHER.

Whole Bottles

MOST COMMONLY, BOTTLES ARE USED TO STORE DRINKS. THE CLOSED BOTTLES
PROTECT THE DRINK AGAINST IMPURITIES SUCH AS BACTERIA AND PREVENT THE
CONTENT FROM EVAPORATING. MANY BOTTLES ARE MADE FROM TINTED GLASS
TO PROTECT THE BEVERAGE AGAINST SUNLIGHT, IN PARTICULAR UV RAYS.

AND OF COURSE THERE ARE ALSO BOTTLES FOR HOUSEHOLD USE (FOR INSTANCE,
FOR SAFELY STORING CLEANING PRODUCTS), AND BOTTLES ARE ALSO USED
IN THE CHEMICAL INDUSTRY. THESE BOTTLES GENERALLY HAVE A WIDER
BOTTLENECK, WHICH ALLOWS USE WITH POWDER OR OTHER SOLIDS.

White Beauty

MATERIALS:
WHOLE BOTTLE, MASKING TAPE,
SPRAY PAINT

YOU CAN MAKE REALLY CHIC VASES QUICKLY AND EASILY. THE VASES IN WHITE
HAVE AN ELEGANT APPEARANCE THAT DOESN'T COMPETE WITH THE FLORAL
DISPLAY, ALLOWING ALL KINDS OF FLOWERS AND GRASSES TO SHINE IN THEM.
KEEP A LOOKOUT FOR BOTTLES WITH PARTICULARLY CONCAVE BOTTOMS.

1. Stick masking tape onto the cleaned bottles. Press down the edges so that no paint will run under the tape.

2. Place the bottle on paper or another protective surface and spay-paint it in a well-ventilated area. Then allow the paint to dry well.

When dry, carefully remove the tape. If the bottle has a particularly beautiful concave bottom, then leave the lower area free from paint.

Pretty in Pastels

MATERIALS:
WHOLE BOTTLE, CHALK PAINT, SMALL
SPONGE OR BRUSH, GOLD LEAF, ADHESIVE,
BRUSH, (OPTIONAL) TWEEZERS

THESE VASES ARE JUST RIGHT FOR EVERYONE WHO ENJOYS PASTEL SHADES.
DABBED WITH CHALK PAINT, THE GLASS BOTTLE TAKES ON A UNIQUE TEXTURE,
AND EVEN THE APPLIED GOLD LEAF HAS A MUCH MORE THREE-DIMENSIONAL
APPEARANCE.

1. Once the labels have been removed from the bottles, dab the bottle with the chalk paint. Then allow it to dry completely.

2. Adhere the gold leaf to the bottle using a brush and a suitable adhesive.

Tweezers may be helpful because the gold leaf is so delicate that it rips if you handle it too roughly. Plus, tweezers help you avoid getting sticky fingers.

When it's fully dried, you can go over the whole bottle with a varnish to better protect the gold leaf.

Get the Jungle Look!

RUMBLE IN THE JUNGLE! THE DECOUPAGE TECHNIQUE IS VERY WELL SUITED FOR GLASS BOTTLES. YOU CAN STICK ON MOTIFS OF YOUR CHOICE AND CREATE TRUE WORKS OF ART—OR EVEN YOUR OWN JUNGLE.

1. To get the decoupage look, you must first paint the bottle white so that you can show off the motifs. Make sure the bottle is completely dry before you begin the decoupage stage.

Neatly cut out the napkin motifs with scissors or tear them out, depending on the pattern you're using and whether you want to have any overlap.

2. Lift off the top layer of the napkin's two or three layers. Only this thin layer will be used.

3. Position the motif where you want it and lightly hold it in place. Use a brush to carefully distribute the decoupage medium from the center outward toward the edges of the motif.

4. When all the design elements have been stuck on and are dried, you can give the whole bottle another layer of decoupage medium.

Vollmundig
Harmonisch
Samtig im
Abgang
Kräftige Note
Feines
Bouquet
Alles Liebe
und Gute
um Geburtstag
von deinen
Jungs

Painted Bottles

IF YOU HAVE BEAUTIFUL HANDWRITING, YOU CAN WRITE ON PAINTED BOTTLES USING A PAINT OR CHALK MARKER. THIS QUICKLY CREATES A COORDINATING OR PERSONALIZED VASE WHEN GIVING FLOWERS AS A GIFT.

Gitti

Martina

Katja

Sibylle

BLACK BEAUTIES. BOTTLES LOOK VERY ELEGANT
IN BLACK ACCESSORIZED WITH A SMALL TAG OR A
HANDMADE LABEL ATTACHED TO THE BOTTLE USING
SEALING WAX.

Bottle Jacket

WHEN IT GETS REALLY FROSTY OUTSIDE, A BOTTLE MIGHT ENJOY COZYING UP IN A JACKET. WHY NOT GIVE VASES A WARM WRAP TOO?

Caught in the Nets

MATERIALS:
BULBOUS BOTTLE, SCISSORS,
JUTE TWINE, HOT-GLUE GUN

MACRAMÉ WAS FASHIONABLE DECADES AGO AND NOW HAS COME BACK! THE LITTLE KNOTS WORK WELL WITH ALL TYPES OF CORD AND YARN, NO MATTER THE MATERIAL OR THE WEIGHT. AND MACRAMÉ IS ACTUALLY NOT ALL THAT DIFFICULT.

1. For this project 12 long cords are attached to a base cord, which you tie around the bottle-neck. Loop a long strand under the base cord. The loop should be facing downward. Then pull cords 1 and 2 over the base and through the loop. Once attached to the base, the cords should be at least twice as long as the height of the bottle. Do this for all 12 cords.

2. Then you start the knots. Each knot is made using four cords. The first knot starts from the left. Place cord 1 *over* cords 2 and 3, and *under* cord 4. Then move cord 4 to the left, *under* cords 2 and 3 and *over* cord 1. Pull lightly. Repeat this process from the right side. That is, you're starting the second knot from the right.

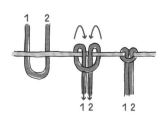

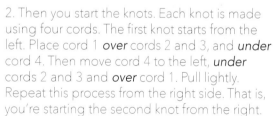

1ST KNOT (STARTING FROM THE LEFT)

Continued on the next page

3. Now take the neighboring pair of cords and knot them in the same way. One knot is sufficient here.

4. In the next round, you knot the neighboring pair of cords again. You continue in this way until the whole bottle is covered in a net.

5. On the final round, you may again wish to tie a double set of knots. Then all the remaining cord ends are brought together at the bottom of the bottle.

If possible, you can tie them up and stick in place using a hot-glue gun.

There can be a bit of tangle underneath the bottle, so if the cord is very thick, you should ensure in advance that the bottle has a very concave bottom in which you can hide the ends.

IF YOU DON'T FEEL LIKE LEARNING SPECIAL KNOTS, YOU CAN INSTEAD JUST USE SIMPLE KNOTS TO DECORATE A BOTTLE. TO DO IT, TAKE TWO CORDS AND TIE THEM TOGETHER AS A DOUBLE STRAND.

Wrap Around

YOU CAN MAKE THIS DESIGN VERY QUICKLY. ALLOW THE PAINTED BOTTLE TO DRY AND THEN WRAP COLORED COTTON CORD AROUND IT. AND VOILÀ!

Stripes and Stars

MATERIALS:
SMALL WHOLE BOTTLES, STICKERS OR
MASKING TAPE, FROSTED-GLASS-EFFECT
SPRAY PAINT

IT LOOKS LIKE FROSTED GLASS. BUT IT'S SPRAY PAINT THAT CREATES THIS EASY YET MAGICAL EFFECT, PERFECT FOR HOLIDAY DECORATION OR FOR WHEN YOU WOULD PREFER A BOTTLE TO BE LESS TRANSPARENT.

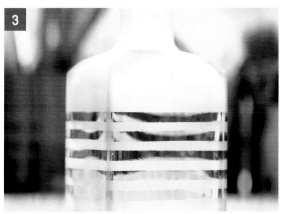

1. First clean a small bottle well and stick the masking tape in place to mask off your pattern. Set the bottle on a protected surface and spray it in a well-ventilated area.

2. Once it has dried (pay attention to the manufacturer's instructions), carefully pull away the masking tape.

3-4. Thin masking tape or small star stickers work well to make contemporary Christmas patterns. But you can do anything you like. The stickers need to be well adhered so that no paint runs under the edges.

Metallics

GOLD IS GREAT, BUT BOTTLES CAN ALSO MAKE OTHER METALLIC STATEMENTS.

Garden Minis

PRETTY HIGHLIGHTS ON THE FENCE: SMALL BOTTLES CAN DECORATE THE PATIO OR THE BALCONY FOR PARTIES.

WHEN THE BIG BOUQUET IS NO LONGER AS FRESH AS IT ONCE WAS, YOU CAN DISPLAY INDIVIDUAL FLOWERS IN SMALL VASES. SMALL BOTTLES ARE PERFECT MINI VASES.

Surface Finish

WHETHER MARBLING IS ON TREND OR NOT IS OF NO IMPORTANCE. IT'S ALWAYS ATTRACTIVE, ESPECIALLY IF YOU CAN CREATE THIS MARBLING EFFECT YOURSELF, AND IN THE COLOR COMBINATIONS THAT YOU LIKE THE BEST.

1. Fill an old plastic bowl with water. Pour in a little of the first color of nail polish. Then add the second color of nail polish and mix a little with a small stick to create a marble pattern.

2. Slowly dunk the bottle into the mix, turn it a little, and pull it back out.

When using this method, make sure that your room is well ventilated. If needed, have some nail polish remover on hand in case of drips.

3. To dry, place the bottles or jars on a piece of old paper. So that the nail polish doesn't stick, place a small wooden block under the bottle or jar.

Rough around the Edges

MATERIALS:
WHOLE BOTTLE, NEWSPAPER, TAPE, SCISSORS,
SMALL BOWL, WALLPAPER PASTE, BRUSH,
SPRAY PAINT (CHALK FINISH), ACRYLIC PAINT

YOU WOULD NEVER GUESS THIS VASE IS AN OLD BOTTLE. AMAZING! YOU DON'T EVEN HAVE TO REMOVE THE LABELS FOR THIS PROJECT BECAUSE EVERYTHING IS HIDDEN. AND WHAT'S REALLY GREAT IS THAT IT'S ACTUALLY VERY LIGHT ALTHOUGH IT LOOKS SO ROBUST.

1. In the first step, you crumple away! Simply place some newspaper around the bottle and fix in place with some tape. Keep moving and resticking it until you have a shape you like.

2. Then paint it with some wallpaper paste and cut some more newspaper into small pieces. Use a brush to stick these pieces to the vase, building up layers.

After three layers, let it dry. Once it's dry, you can test how stable the surface is. The more layers added, the firmer the vase will be.

Continued on the next page

3. Once enough layers have been applied and they have dried, you can apply paint to the vase. In this case, chalk spray paint was used.

4. Now you can add designs or simply fill a brush with white acrylic paint and splatter the vase. Finally, add a coat of varnish to protect the vase against drips when you fill it up.

A COOL ALTERNATIVE IS TO ADD A FINAL LAYER OF NEWSPAPER AND THEN LEAVE THE VASE UNPAINTED; SIMPLY SEAL IT WITH A COAT OF VARNISH.

Small Magic Lantern

MATERIALS:
SMALL BOTTLE, LAMP WICK, WICK
HOLDER SET, LAMP OIL, PAINT OR CHALK
MARKER

OIL LAMPS BURN BETTER WHEN THERE'S A LITTLE BREEZE. THIS SMALL OIL LAMP IS QUICKLY MADE AND CAN BE VERY QUICKLY REFILLED.

1. Clean the bottle well and decorate or write on it using a paint or chalk marker.

2. Collect all the parts for the finished lamp.

3. Pour in the lamp oil using a small funnel.

4. Now assemble the wick holder set according to the manufacturer's instructions and place it in the bottleneck.

Water Plants

FLOWERS, SMALL TWIGS, GRASSES—THESE PLANTS
LAST A SURPRISINGLY LONG TIME IN WATER WHEN
THE BOTTLE IS SEALED AT THE TOP WITH A CANDLE.
THEY DEFINITELY MAKE YOU LOOK TWICE.

GENIE IN THE BOTTLE. FAIRY LIGHTS THAT YOU CAN SIMPLY INSERT INTO A BOTTLE ARE EFFORT-FREE. ADD A LITTLE DECORATION TO THE BOTTLE AND YOU HAVE A QUICK AND ATMOSPHERIC LIGHT.

Washed Up by the Tide

MATERIALS:
BULBOUS BOTTLE, SAND, SMALL SHELL,
"SECRET MESSAGE," TREASURE MAP OR
COUPON, STOPPER, (OPTIONAL) TWINE

A MESSAGE IN A BOTTLE WITH A TREASURE MAP. THIS BOTTLE LOOKS TOO GOOD TO OPEN TO GET OUT THE MAP! BUT WHAT IF THIS BOTTLE WERE AN ELABORATE WAY TO GIVE A GIFT COUPON? THEN SOMEONE WOULD HAVE FUN FISHING IT OUT!

1. The bottle should be clean and dry on the inside. You can decorate the bottleneck with some twine.

2. Use a funnel to pour in the sand. Place small shells, pebbles, or pieces of driftwood into the bottle on top of the sand.

3. And, of course, don't forget to insert the secret message, treasure map, or gift coupon.

Stick in the cork! Try to keep from shaking this.

Yummy Yummy!

MATERIALS:
WHOLE BOTTLE, CUT WOOD, WOOD GLUE,
ROPE, CORD STOPPER, DRILL, SAW, SCREW-
DRIVER, WOOD SCREWS, VARNISH, BRUSH

"PLEASE FEED US!" WHEN THE WINTERS ARE COLD AND FROSTY, WE CAN HELP OUR FEATHERED FRIENDS. A FEEDING STATION IS ALWAYS VERY WELCOME, AND IT'S ALSO A JOY TO WATCH THE LITTLE BIRDS FEAST ON THE FOOD.

Cut-wood sizes needed:
1 × (6 × 16 in.) 0.75 in. thick – back
1 × (6 × 6.5 in.) 0.75 in. thick – base
1 × (6 × 4.75 in.) 0.75 in. thick – roof piece 1
1 × (5 × 4.75 in.) 0.75 in. thick – roof piece 2
3 × (0.75 × 4.75 in.) 0.75 in. thick – tray

Bottle holder is made from the back's offcuts.

See the next page for assembly diagram.

For this project, an old board was used, so its width—6 in.—is what I based the above measurements on.

1. The longest board must be sawn off at the top corners at 45°. Then glue or screw the base (6 x 6.5 in.) and the back (6 x 16 in.) together.

2. Make the bottle holder from the offcuts of roof corners. Saw off a piece so it will lie flush with the side of the back piece, and stick it in place so that bottle floats a little above the base, allowing the food to drop through easily.

To the right and left of the bottle in the upper third of the back, drill two holes for the rope.

Continued on the next page

3. Glue or screw on the roof.

4. Now all that's missing is the tray for the bird food. To make it, simply stick the three battens in place on the base.

If the feeding station will be exposed to the wind and rain, then it should be protected with a coat of varnish suitable for outdoor use.

Fill up the bottle with the bird food. Close the lid and position it in the feeding station. Use a rope to attach the bottle at the top: Feed the rope through the holes to the right and left of the bottle and pull together on the back with a cord stopper. This allows the rope to be easily loosened to remove the bottle for refills. Alternatively, a rubber band could be used.

Now, remove the bottle lid and let the birds enjoy their food.

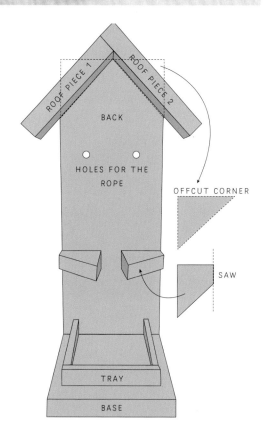

IF YOU WANT TO GIVE THE FOOD TRAY A LITTLE MORE PROTECTION, YOU CAN CREATE A SMALL COVER BY STICKING SOME BATTEN OFFCUTS OVER THE EDGES. THE CORNERS OF THE BATTENS SHOULD HAVE MITER JOINTS.

LEMON
BODYSCRUB

HANDMADE WITH
SUGAR & LOVE

LAVENDER
BODYSCRUB

HANDMADE WITH
SUGAR & LOVE

LEMON
BODYSCRUB

HANDMADE WITH
SUGAR & LOVE

LAVENDER
BODYSCRUB

HANDMADE WITH
SUGAR & LOVE

PORCELAIN

PETRA KNOBLAUCH

Introduction

"Life is colorful!"

And for me, becoming a china fan was also a colorful journey. I've spent half my life looking at shapes, colors, trends, and patterns, and deciding if they are "in" or "out." It's part of my day job as a fashion editor. From there it's just a small step away: tableware is also about colors and shapes, and ultimately whether something is "in" (i.e., whether it corresponds to the zeitgeist), or whether it's "out" and should be thrown away.

Small amounts of china can very easily and legally be disposed of in domestic waste, while large amounts end up in the dumpster designated for construction rubble at the landfill. Not a happy end for the material, which is sometimes called "white gold" because it is expensive to produce, and as a result it can be very valuable. "Use everything. Waste nothing" is my motto, and porcelain is precisely where sustainability comes into play for me. For my work as a mosaic artist, it doesn't matter whether the china is currently on trend. I have a thing for pretty shards, chipped plates, and odd dishes. Be it little flowers, checks, or 1970s or 1950s style, they all inspire my mosaic work. So I also call my work "upcycling art"—the process of making new from old.

On the following pages, I'll guide you through the colorful world of recycling china. With innumerable crafting ideas for beginners and more advanced makers, I want to entice you to create small and large porcelain projects. Maybe you too will develop a love for it and can save a few pieces of china from the trash.

A Passion for Porcelain

Are you a passionate collector? Have you found unimagined china treasures in the attic? Or are your dishes simply due for an update? In the pages ahead you'll find the best tips and projects.

As an article of daily use, china is naturally also a reflection of its time and has always been adapted to suit respective lifestyles. In the 1950s and '60s, coffee and tea services were still in use, but nowadays everyone has their own personal coffee mug. Tea and coffee have long been poured directly into cups from the kettle or the coffee machine, rendering tea and coffeepots superfluous. The same can be said for creamers and sugar bowls, because milk now comes from the frother, and sugar from packets. It all means that many pretty pieces of china are no longer in use.

China is also subject to the various trends. The typical '70s colors, shapes, and patterns were replaced by the purism of the '80s and '90s. To match the simple yet elegant presentation of nouvelle cuisine, the decoration on the plates also had to be minimalistic. Back then, it was also preferable for the plates to have eight sides and to be plain black.

Whether your china is no longer fashionable, showing signs of wear, not a full set, or simply no longer of any use, it is definitely too much of a shame to throw away these unique pieces.

For this book, we created over 50 different china projects and saved the pieces from going to the dump. Sometimes, a coat of paint or new contents is enough, and other times flair and artisanal skill are needed to create an exclusive porcelain object.

Upcycling art—ever heard of it? The combination of the words "up" and "recycling" implies that the items are reused and something better is made from them. It means that you can be proud of your work, with good reason.

Techniques

For the dozens of creative projects in this section, I've used a truly varied assortment of materials and techniques. I tried some of the techniques for the first time when writing this book. Some of them are easy, while others take more skill. A tip: use "test plates" when you're trying a new technique, so you can get a feeling for the various paints, transfer foils, pastes, and adhesives.

Chalkboard paint:
Is quickly applied and guarantees a real wow effect. The paint covers so well that you can also paint over any unattractive patterns.

Marbling paints:
Marbling paints are popular, and that's no surprise because creating magical marble effects is child's play and it's a lot of fun. Acrylic paints aren't food-safe and should be used only for decoration. If you want to experiment, you can try out the technique by using nail polish.

Creative concrete:
Concrete paste can be used really easily when you follow the manufacturer's instructions. Its appearance is very close to "real" concrete. It was something new for me, since I use a special cement-sand mixture for my mosaics.

Porcelain markers:
They work like felt tips: shake, press the tip, and draw. I think these pens are perfect for writing on porcelain. They are well suited for children to draw on china too. The ink is baked in the oven to dry and is food-safe and dishwasher safe.

Kintsugi:
This adhesive art is originally from Japan and translates to mean "golden repair." A kintsugi kit consists of two-component epoxy, gold powder, a putty to fill in missing areas, disposable gloves, and wooden applicator sticks. You mix the epoxy with the gold powder and apply the paste thickly to one of the edges so that the repaired break will be more noticeable.

Transfer foils:
Making transfer images yourself is great fun. Three-dimensional objects are photographed and then brought onto the transfer sheet with a laser printer. The created transfer image is then applied to the china.

Concrete-effect paint:
Simple and effective. The paint is ready to go, so you can start work with it immediately. It's a great idea; in the vase project here I decided on a thick, rough layer, but you can also apply it more sparingly and sand down the finish.

Gold leaf:
Little effort, great effect. Gold leaf lends any piece of china a glamorous touch and is very easy to work with.

Hanging a Plate

Out of the kitchen cupboard and up onto the wall. Many creative projects liberate plates from their existence in the darkest corner of a cupboard and turn them into wall decorations. Here are a few tips for finding the correct mount for each newly designed plate.

I tried the popular internet DIY tip of using a glue gun to stick paper clips or can tabs to a plate for hanging. It looked possible, but unfortunately it didn't work for me.

Plate Hanger
This way of hanging a plate is a relic from the 1950s, when plates depicting scenes were popular vacation souvenirs. The plates evoked happy memories while hanging safely, usually on the kitchen wall. The advantage is that the springs in the plate hangers are very flexible and work well for many different sizes of plate. A small drawback is that the little "claws" can be seen on the front of the plate.

Adhesive Plate Hanger
The adhesive hanger is a very cheap option to hang a plate, and you can buy them in various sizes at the hardware store. A small triangular metal loop is affixed to the plate with material coated with adhesive. You dampen the material and press it against the plate. Beware: usually these must dry for 24 hours before hanging. Its advantage is that it's a very easy and invisible way to hang a plate.

Decorative Hanging
This works only for plates that have holes around the rim, but it looks particularly decorative. Thread a thin ribbon through the holes, tie together, and voilà.

Holes in the China
Valuable ornamental plates should not be used on the table but were primarily intended as wall decoration. Many china manufacturers worked two holes into the back of the plates to guarantee that they could be safely hung. Thread a wire through the holes and form a loop that points to the top of the plate, then weave the ends together under the holes.

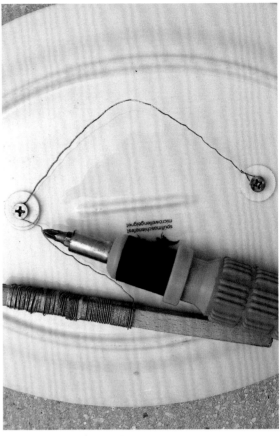

Plate Stands

Plate stands offer an alternative way to present plates. Their advantage is that no hammer or nails are required, and the plates can be swapped out at any time. Plate stands come in all sizes and materials.

Wire Hanger

If you've drilled holes into the china as part of your project, you can easily use them to hang the plate. Washers are important; screw in the screws only after the washers are in place, and ensure that you leave enough room for the wire. Decide on the length of the hanger and then weave the ends of the wire between the washer and the screw several times.

Plates by the Pile

BE THEY CHIPPED OR DISCARDED, OR YOU ARE SIMPLY SICK OF THE SIGHT OF THEM,
YOUR CUPBOARDS OFTEN HOLD TREASURES THAT ARE JUST WAITING TO BE BROUGHT
BACK TO LIFE.

THEY COULD BE CAKE PLATES OR LARGE DINING PLATES WITH INTRICATE PATTERNS
OR JUST PLAIN WHITE; INDIVIDUAL PIECES OR A SET; PLATES ASSOCIATED WITH MANY
MEMORIES OR THAT HAVE SMALL DEFECTS. IT'S A CRYING SHAME TO SIMPLY THROW
THEM OUT. USING PAINT, INTUITION, AND IMAGINATION, YOU CAN CREATE SMALL ART-
WORKS THAT WILL GIVE YOU PLEASURE FOR A LONG TIME. EVEN IF SOMETHING BREAKS
BY ACCIDENT, IT CAN BE PUT BACK TOGETHER TO MAKE A UNIQUE ORNAMENT. THE
GERMAN SAYING IS TRUE: "SHARDS BRING GOOD LUCK."

Golden Repairs

MATERIALS:
PORCELAIN, TWO-PART EPOXY, GOLD POWDER,
WOODEN APPLICATOR STICK, DISPOSABLE
GLOVES, PLASTIC LID

SOMETIMES A FAVORITE PIECE OF CHINA GETS BROKEN, AND YOU DESPERATELY WANT TO REPAIR IT. YOU CAN USE NORMAL PORCELAIN GLUE, OR YOU CAN TRY THE DECORATIVE KINTSUGI METHOD. THE TREND IS ORIGINALLY FROM JAPAN AND TRANSLATES AS "GOLDEN REPAIR."

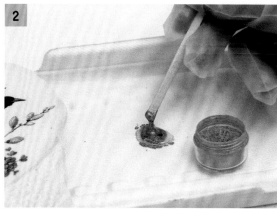

1. Collect your supplies on a suitable work surface. Put on the disposable gloves and break the china.

2. Squeeze out the two-component epoxy on the lid, making sure that there is enough to cover the break. (Alternatively, you can use a kintsugi kit.)

Add the (very fine) gold dust to the glue. A small amount will be enough.

3. Use the wooden applicator stick to generously apply the glue to the broken edge of one part of the plate.

4. Place the second part of the broken plate on the glue mixture and gently press together. To dry, position the plate with the front side facing down. Unfortunately, if you press the two pieces together with too much force, other breaks can occur that will need to be mended . . .

Goldsmith

MATERIALS:
BROKEN CHINA, (OPTIONAL) TILE NIPPERS AND PROTECTIVE GLOVES, CORKS, SUITABLE LOOP OR EYELET FOR PENDANTS, AND A KINTSUGI SET, OR ALTERNATIVELY: TWO-COMPONENT EPOXY, VERY FINE GOLD POWDER, WOODEN APPLICATOR STICK, DISPOSABLE GLOVES, LID

YOU DON'T HAVE TO BE A GOLDSMITH TO DESIGN THESE UNIQUE PIECES OF JEWELRY. ALL YOU NEED ARE SHARDS OF CHINA, LOOPS OR EYELETS, EPOXY, AND GOLD DUST.

1. If you don't have any suitable shards of china at the ready, put on the protective gloves and place the nippers next to the desired motif on the plate and press. In this way, slowly work around the motif to cut it out. Plates with pretty patterns are particularly suitable for this project.

2. Put on the disposable gloves. Squeeze the two-component epoxy onto the lid and mix in a small amount of the gold dust. Use the applicator stick to generously spread the glue around the broken edges of the shard.

3. Now place the shard onto the cork, with the motif side facing downward. This allows beautiful golden drops to form.

4. When the "gold mount" has dried, glue the eyelet or loop onto the back of the shard. You can use superglue.

Parade of Plates

THIS BOARD WITH COAT HOOKS OFFERS ONCE-LOVED PLATES A PLACE FOR DISPLAY WHILE BEING USEFUL. TO AVOID UGLY DRILL HOLES IN THE CENTER OF THE PLATES, THE PRETTY CHINA IS ATTACHED WITH SIMPLE ADHESIVE PLATE HANGERS.

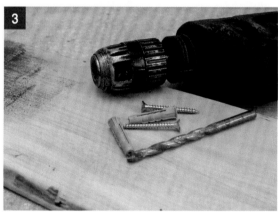

1. First affix the plate hangers to the back of the plates. Note: the drying time is approximately 24 hours.

2. Collect your materials and lay out a drop cloth. Paint the board (approximately 34 × 6.5 in.). The paint used here is matte and quick drying.

3. Drill the holes in the board so that it can be attached to the wall. Make sure to position the holes so that later they are covered by the plates.

Position the plates (in this example, four cake plates and a small saucer) on the board and mark where the nails should go for hanging the plates. Make sure there is enough space at the bottom of the board for the hooks. Hammer the nails into the board.

4. Position the plates on the board again and mark where the coat hooks should go. Remove the plates and hammer in the hooks.

Use screws and wall plugs to hang the board in the desired place on the wall. Then hang the plates on it.

ALWAYS CLOSE AT HAND: YOUR MOST BEAUTIFUL OR IMPORTANT KITCHEN UTENSILS NOW HAVE A NEW HOME! CHOOSE THE SIZE AND COLOR OF THE BOARD TO MATCH YOUR STYLE.

Neatly Tied Up

MATERIALS:
PLATES AND SMALL BOWLS WITH HOLES
AROUND THE RIM, THIN RIBBON

A FRESH TAKE ON ROMANTIC ORNAMENTAL PLATES WITH HOLES AROUND THE RIM: THE BRIGHT RIBBON IS WOVEN THROUGH THE DELICATE PATTERN OF HOLES.

Starting at the top of the plate, thread the ribbon through the hole pattern. Tie the two ends together close to the plate and make a

loop that can be used to hang the plate. A bow can be added separately if you like.

CHEERFUL BRIGHT ACCENTS: ON THEIR OWN OR IN SMALL GROUPS, THESE CHINA PLATES ARE AN UNUSUAL EYE-CATCHER.

Welcome

WELCOME TO THE MOSAIC FACTORY! MAYBE YOUR FAVORITE DISHES GOT BROKEN THE LAST TIME YOU MOVED? MAYBE YOU HAVE SOME BORING PLATES THAT ARE DESPERATELY CALLING OUT TO BE RECYCLED? THEN THIS CREATIVE PROJECT IS FOR YOU.

1. First break the china. Wear protective gloves and safety glasses. Line the tub with newspaper and hit the center of the china with a hammer. The random shards of china become the filling material for the heart. Now use the nippers to shape the shards into the shapes you need. First remove the rim of the plate; these rim pieces will become the outer pieces of the heart mosaic.

Also "cut out" the flower motif. Nip around the motif as if you were working with scissors.

2. On a firm surface, draw the outline of the silicon heart-shaped cake mold. Arrange the shards in the outline, starting with the plate edges.

Remember to leave enough space for two holes in order to be able to hang up the mosaic later.

Among the shards, position the letter beads to read "Welcome" or another message.

3. Put on safety glasses and disposable gloves. Measure the cement mix and water according to the instructions on the package and mix them together in the old bowl. For the heart you'll need approximately 2.2 lbs. of cement mix powder. Knead the mixture into a ball until it has the consistency of pastry dough.

4. To allow unmolding of the cement later, coat the silicon heart-shaped mold with oil. Quickly spread the cement mixture in the silicon heart.

It's important that the cement molding mixture has a smooth and even surface. Depending on the manufacturer, the cement molding material

can be worked for 45 to 60 minutes. After that it becomes too stiff.

5. Start with the edges of the heart and press the shards from the rim of the plate into the cement molding material. Begin working around the upper contours of the heart. For the hanging holes, simply insert straws in the desired positions. Also position the flower motif and the letter beads. Leave a distance of approximately 0.25 to 0.75 in. between the individual pieces of the mosaic. Press everything in well to avoid any unevenness. If the gap between the individual shards is too big, then use the pliers to create smaller pieces to fit in the gap.

Depending on the manufacturer of the cement molding material, it should be fully dry in approximately 24 hours. You can use a putty knife to remove any jagged edges.

The cement molding material can be easily removed from the silicone mold.

6. Now for the sanding. Use fine sandpaper to rub away any remaining roughness between the shards. The letters can be cleaned with a toothpick. Wipe down with a damp towel. Finally, thread the cord through the holes to hang it up.

MINE SAYS "COME IN!" A UNIQUE PRESENT FOR A GERMAN-SPEAKING FRIEND'S HOUSEWARMING PARTY.

HEREINSPAZIERT

In Keeping with the Times

MATERIALS:
2 PLATES, DRILL, DIAMOND-TIP BIT,
MASKING TAPE, CLOCK KIT

ONCE UPON A TIME, CLOCKS HUNG IN EVERY LIVING ROOM. NOW, WE'RE ONCE AGAIN IN LOVE WITH THE RETRO CHARM OF AN ANALOG TIMEPIECE, ESPECIALLY IF IT'S MADE FROM OLD PLATES.

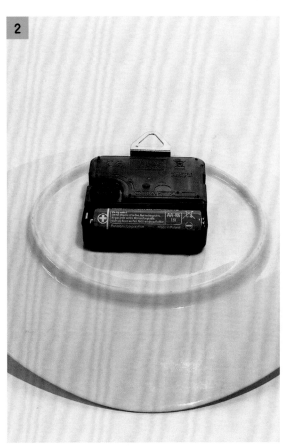

1. To attach the hands in front of the plates and the clockwork behind them, you will need to drill a hole in the center of the plates. To do this, find a firm surface and lightly pad it with an old towel. Now decide on the positions of the holes and mark with masking tape on both sides of the plate.

Put on protective gloves and start drilling through the plate from the pattern side. Drill briefly, then put a little water in the dent you made, to prevent the drill from becoming too hot.

2. Once both plates have a hole in the middle, you work from the back side of the clock.

Attach a hanger to the clock kit and then position the components as follows on the small thread screw of the clock kit: the large plate, a washer, and finally the small plate on top of the washer. Use the supplied nut to screw both of the plates as well as the clock kit together. Now attach the hands. Insert the battery.

Neon Marble

THE HEIGHT OF LUXURY: CHARGERS GIVE ANY TABLE A TOUCH OF CLASS. THEY ALSO LOOK VERY MODERN WHEN THEY'RE DECORATED USING A MARBLING TECHNIQUE WITH NEON PAINTS. THE UNIQUE RESULTS ARE ALWAYS A SURPRISE AND A GOOD IDEA ON YOUR TABLE.

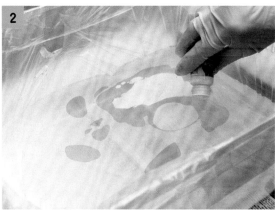

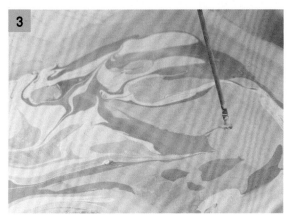

1. Cover your workspace with some old newspaper and collect your materials. Fill a bowl with cold water. If you don't have an old bowl, the best way to protect your vessel is to line it with a plastic garbage bag.

2. Shake the paints well (I used white, rose, and neon orange). Put on the disposable gloves and add the paint drop by drop to the surface of the water.

Start with the main color, pink in my example. Then add the first decorative color, neon orange in my case. Last, add some white accents.

3. Use the sticks to mix the paints so that a marble pattern is created.

4. Now dip the plates in the mixture. Holding the plate carefully with both hands, slide into the water and back out. Blow away any excess water or, alternatively, carefully wipe it off with a paper towel.

After approximately eight hours, the plate should be completely dry.

After you've marbled the plate, carefully soak up the excess paint from the used water with a paper towel before discarding the water.

The paint used here is not food-safe.

QUICK AND EASY: THIS IS A JAZZY SPRING MAKEOVER FOR TABLE DÉCOR.

Piled High

MATERIALS:
4 DIFFERENT CAKE PLATES OR SAUCERS, A
SET OF CAKE STAND LEGS WITH WASHERS,
DRILL, DIAMOND-TIP BIT, MASKING TAPE,
RULER, PENCIL, PROTECTIVE GLOVES

CREATIVE RECYCLING—WHEN COMBINING DAINTY PLATES AND SAUCERS, THERE'S NO LIMIT TO YOUR IMAGINATION. COLORS AND PATTERNS CAN BE MIXED AS YOU LIKE. THIS CAKE STAND HAS A PARTICULARLY PLEASING SHAPE IF THE PLATES ARE SMALLER TOWARD THE TOP.

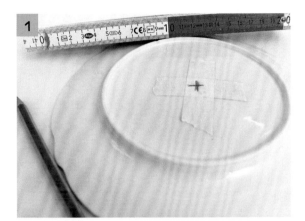

1. Drill a hole in the center of all the plates for the cake stand legs. To do this, find a firm surface and lightly pad with an old towel. Now decide on the positions of the holes, using a ruler, and mark them with masking tape and pencil on both sides of the plates.

2. Put on the protective gloves and start drilling through the plates from the pattern side. Drill briefly, then put a little water in the dent you made, to prevent the drill from becoming too hot.

Prepare all four plates in the same way.

3. Connect the plates in size order using the cake stand legs. When doing so, always place a washer on the top and bottom of each plate.

Together Forever

MATERIALS:
2 WHITE PLATES, AN OLD BOWL, PAPER TO
USE AS DROP CLOTH, DISPOSABLE GLOVES,
WOODEN STICKS, PAPER TOWELS, MARBLING
PAINT, PENCIL, PORCELAIN MARKERS

TWO ODD PLATES NOW BELONG TOGETHER. A THOUGHTFUL WEDDING GIFT CAN
BE CREATED IN TWO STEPS: MARBLING FOLLOWED BY LETTERING.

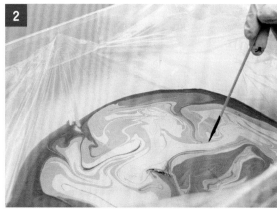

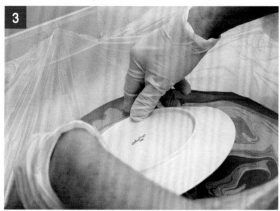

1. Cover your workspace with some old newspaper and collect your materials. Fill a bowl with cold water. If you don't have an old bowl, the best way to protect your vessel is to line it with a plastic garbage bag.

Shake the paints well (I used white, gray, and neon pink). Put on disposable gloves and add the paint drop by drop to the surface of the water.

Start with the main color; in this example it's gray. Then add the first decorative color, in this example neon pink. Finally add some white accents.

2. Use a stick to mix the individual colors as you like so that a marble pattern is created.

3. Now dip the plates in the mixture. Holding the plate carefully with both hands, slide into the water and back out. Blow away any excess water or, alternatively, carefully wipe it off with a paper towel.

After you have marbled the plate, carefully soak up the excess paint from the used water with a paper towel before discarding the water.

4. After approximately eight hours, the plate should be completely dry. Now you can write on the marble pattern. Carefully draw the letters with a pencil, then trace over them with a porcelain marker.

The paint used here is not food-safe.

What's New?

Kiss

Gone
to see
Jonas

Friday
7 o'clock
R + N

WE ALL HAVE A COUPLE OF ODD PLATES THAT ARE JUST TOO NICE TO THROW AWAY. HUNG UP TOGETHER, THEY CAN MAKE A UNIQUE NOTICE BOARD THAT WON'T BE OVERLOOKED!

This method works best when you use bright plates or plates with a colored rim. You can also use serving plates or cake plates. The important thing is that the center of the plate is flat. The plates should be clean. Lay out some newspaper to catch drips, and off you go!

1. Shake the bottle of blackboard paint well, then put some paint in the center of the plate and use a brush to spread it in a circle. The paint will go a long way, so use it sparingly.

2. You can get an even finish to the circle edge by placing the brush next to the plate rim and then slowly turning the plate under it. The circle will be perfect only if you use a template. Paint all of the center and leave it to dry for four days.

Mirror, Mirror on the Wall

MATERIALS:
WHITE PORCELAIN PLATE, MIRROR
THE SAME SIZE AS THE CENTER OF
THE PLATE, WIDE DOUBLE-SIDED TAPE,
PORCELAIN PAINT IN NEON PINK AND
NEON GREEN, PLATE HANGER

ANY PLATES WITH HOLES AROUND THE RIMS CAN BE UPCYCLED IN NO TIME WITH A LITTLE PAINT. PERKED UP WITH AN OLD HAND MIRROR, THEY BECOME UNIQUE WALL DECORATIONS.

As with any painting on china, plates should be clean and dry. It's best to first test the porcelain marker on the back of the plate. It should work like a felt tip; shake well first and then depress the tip.

Before drawing, take a moment to be inspired by the pattern or the structure of the plate. A colorfully painted edge always looks pretty. A structured edge or one with holes in it makes decorating it easier.

Allow the paint on the china to dry for about four hours and then heat the plate in the oven, following the manufacturer's instructions, to make the paint dishwasher safe.

1. The old, maybe even slightly damaged, mirror is given a makeover by writing on it, and it's then stuck onto the plate. Press the double-sided tape onto the back of the mirror and then cut it into shape around the mirror before sticking it in place on the plate. Mirrors from cosmetics packaging, such as eye shadow or blush, work well for saucers.

2. Finally, fit the plate hanger.

Love

GOING TO THE HEART INSTEAD OF THE HIPS—THESE CAKE PLATES KNOW WHAT THEY ARE ABOUT! AND IF YOU HAVE MORE OF THESE LITTLE PLATES, WHY NOT WRITE THE NAMES OF YOUR CHILDREN, "HAPPY FAMILY," OR "GOOD MORNING." INCIDENTALLY, THIS PROJECT IS ALSO GREAT FUN FOR THE KIDS.

1–2. First test the paint on the back of the plate. At the same time, you can also try out different brush shapes.

3. Painting by number: first decide the size of the letters and use the felt tip to make small guide dots for the outlines of the letters.

4. Then join the dots with quick brushstrokes. If a line isn't perfect, you can wipe the paint away with paper towels. You have to be quick with this because the paint dries fast.

Once all the lines are drawn, color them in with paint. As soon as the paint has dried, you can attach the plate hanger to the back of the plates.

#Eat

MATERIALS:
4 DIFFERENT SAUCERS (THEIR CENTERS
SHOULD BE A SINGLE LIGHT COLOR), PLATE
HANGERS, PORCELAIN PAINT, BLACK
PORCELAIN MARKER, BRUSH

DELICATELY DECORATED TEA AND COFFEE SETS WERE THE PRIDE OF GRANNY'S DISPLAY CABINET. KEPT SAFE AND WELL CARED FOR, THEY WERE BROUGHT OUT ONLY ON SPECIAL OCCASIONS. BUT IF A CUP SHOULD BREAK, YOU CAN RECYCLE ITS SAUCER WITH A LITTLE PAINT TO BECOME A BEAUTIFUL WALL DECORATION.

1. The saucers should be clean and dry. For the base color, it's best to choose a paint that matches the pattern on the saucer. It's easy to work without a template because the center always has a slight indent where the cup was placed.

2. Mix the paint well, until it's creamy and easy to work with. To intensify the tone of the paint color, it is best to give the center two coats.

Allow the base paint to dry well. Now use the porcelain marker to write the individual letters on the saucers. It works like a felt tip: before using it for the first time, shake well.

Attach plate hangers to the back of the plates.

Picture Perfect

WE LOVE IT: LITTLE EFFORT, GREAT EFFECT! AN ASSORTMENT OF SAUCERS
WORKS WELL AS UNIQUE PICTURE FRAMES. FOR LARGER PHOTOS, YOU CAN ALSO
USE A NORMAL-SIZED PLATE AS THE FRAME.

1. Place the glass that is the size of the center of
the saucers on the selected photo and draw
around it. Now place the double-sided tape on
the back of the photo and then cut around the
circle drawn on the front of the photo.

2. Pull the protective film off the double-sided
tape and stick the photo in the center of the
saucer and press.

Collection Plates

MATERIALS:
FLAT PLATES, TRANSFER FOILS, LASER
PRINTER, SMALL BOWL FOR WATER,
SCISSORS, PLATE HANGERS, BRUSH,
(OPTIONAL) GOLD LEAF, (OPTIONAL)
MASKING TAPE

USE AN ASSORTMENT OF PLATES TO MAKE YOUR OWN PERSONAL GALLERY. COPY PHOTOS ONTO A SPECIAL TRANSFER FOIL. DEPENDING ON YOUR PERSONAL TASTE, YOU CAN COMBINE THE CREATED TRANSFER WITH PAINT OR GOLD LEAF. IF YOU COMBINE MODERN AND NOSTALGIC PLATES AS A BASE FOR THE MOTIFS, YOU CAN ACHIEVE REALLY INTERESTING EFFECTS.

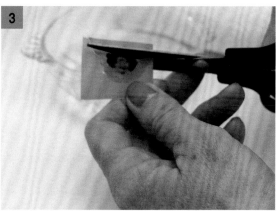

Transfer Foil

1. Select the motif to print on the transfer foil. You can base the motifs on scrapbook images or photos from books, but also 3-D things, such as colorful pom-pons, dolls, teddy bears, shells, feathers, and the like.

2. Simply take a photo of the motif and print it on normal paper. Then place the printed-out images on the laser photocopier and put the transfer sheet in the paper drawer and make a color copy.

3. Cut out the motif carefully and place in a small bowl of lukewarm water for approximately 30 to 60 seconds.

4. When the backing paper curls slightly, you can slide the motif onto the porcelain and position it. Use a paper towel to mop up any excess water and smooth out any air bubbles.

Continued on the
following page

Transfer Foil and Paint

Toadstool Plate

1. To make the red-spotted bottom half, divide an oval plate in half with masking tape. Paint one half red. After it has dried, paint on the white dots. A white porcelain marker makes this easy.

2. Finally, apply the transfer motif (in this case, a full image showing a toadstool), as previously described.

Pom-Pom Plate

A plate with a stripy rim is given a modern coat of paint. Use a wide brush to make quick strokes on the plate rim (see image 1) and apply the transfer motif as previously described.

4. A plate with a colored rim is well suited for painting a rainbow (for example, with acrylic matte paint in pink, turquoise, and carmine). Divide the plate in half with masking tape. Use the curve of the plate as a guide to paint the rainbow.

Allow the paint to dry and then use the next color of paint. Once all the paint has dried, remove the masking tape and apply the motif as previously described.

Tip: Any surface unevenness can be removed with a razor blade.

Transfer Foil and Gold Leaf

1. The plate must be clean. First draw a circle in the center of the plate. Then carefully fill it in using the gilding size and the dark brush.

2. After about 20 minutes, the gilding size will be dry and transparent. Place the gold leaf on the circle and flatten on the plate using a brush. Any excess gold can be carefully removed with the other end of the brush. Allow it all to completely dry for at least 12 hours and then carefully polish it with a soft cloth.

3. Again, leave it to dry for several days, then give it a coat of varnish.

4. Finally place the transfer motifs on the plate (see page 179).

THIS PERSONAL GALLERY IS AN ENCHANTING EYECATCHER. SOUVENIRS FROM YOUR LATEST VACATION OR PLAYFUL SCRAPBOOK IMAGES CAN ALSO BE PRINTED AS TRANSFER MOTIFS.

Refilling Old Cups

THE KITCHEN IS NO LONGER THE HAUNT OF BEAUTIFUL OLD COFFEE CUPS, AT LEAST SINCE THE ADVANCE OF COFFEE CAPSULE MACHINES AND COFFEE MUGS. TYPICAL OF THE 1950S AND '60S, DELICATE PORCELAIN WITH ROMANTIC PATTERNS, ELABORATELY DECORATED HANDLES, AND OF COURSE MATCHING SAUCERS RADIATE THEIR SIMPLE RETRO CHARM. WITH CREATIVE IDEAS AND NEW CONTENTS, THEY CAN TAKE ON A COOL INDUSTRIAL STYLE OR FOLLOW A SHABBY CHIC STYLE.

Drive-Thru for Birds

MATERIALS:
AN ASSORTMENT OF CUPS, TWIGS OR SMALL
STICKS, SECATEURS, CORD FOR HANGING.
FOR THE FOOD: SUNFLOWER HEARTS, ROLLED OATS,
MARGARINE, PAN, STIRRING SPOON.

SERVE UP BIRD FOOD INSTEAD OF COFFEE IN THESE CUPS. THIS SIMPLE
CREATIVE PROJECT IS GREAT FUN, ESPECIALLY FOR SMALL CHILDREN SINCE IT
CAN BE MADE WITHOUT ANY TOOLS.

1. First cut the stick or twig to the right length for the cup. It should extend by 1.5 or 2 in. out of the cup so it can serve as a perch for the birds.

2. Now it's time to get to work in the kitchen. Melt the margarine in the pan. Mix in the oats first and then the sunflower hearts.

3. Position the sticks or twigs opposite the cup handles and use a spoon to fill the cup with the warm bird food. Once the food has cooled down, the stick or twig shouldn't wobble in the food.

Tie the cord to the cup handle and hang in a tree.

TIP:
WRAPPING THE CUP OF BIRD FOOD IN
CELLOPHANE MAKES A THOUGHTFUL GIFT.

Nestcafe

MATERIALS:
COFFEE CUPS WITH SAUCERS, SMALL
PEBBLES OR CLAY FRAGMENTS,
COMPOST OR SOIL, WHEATGRASS SEEDS

THIS PROJECT GIVES A COUPLE OF COFFEE CUPS A TEMPORARY ALTERNATIVE USE. THEY NOT ONLY ARE A NICE WAY TO SERVE YOUR MORNING COFFEE BUT CAN ALSO BE USED AS A NEST FOR EASTER DECORATIONS.

1. Collect your material and place the pebbles or clay fragments in the cups. The pebbles prevent waterlogging, since water can't run out of the cups.

2. Now fill the cup with compost up to about 3 cm from the top of the cup. Scatter the seeds on top and cover with a thin layer of compost.

Place the cup on a well-lit windowsill and water regularly.

After just a few days, you should see green shoots. After about three weeks, there will be a small jungle growing from the cups. Cut the grass and decorate according to your taste.

TIP:
USING A CUP FROM YOUR BREAKFAST SERVICE MAKES THE NEST LOOK ENCHANTING AS A DECORATION FOR YOUR EASTER BREAKFAST.

Kitchen Tidy

MATERIALS:
3 CUPS AND SAUCERS, WOODEN BOARD, WOODEN STICK OF
CORRESPONDING LENGTH, DRILL, DIAMOND-TIP BIT, WOOD
BIT, MASKING TAPE, RULER, 3 NUTS AND BOLTS, 9 WASHERS,
SCREWDRIVER, SAFETY GLASSES, PROTECTIVE GLOVES, 2
SCREWS WITH PLUGS

A NEW JOB FOR OLD ORNAMENTAL CUPS. INSTEAD OF COFFEE AND CREAM, THEY'RE NOW SERVING EVERYDAY KITCHEN UTENSILS.

1. Lightly sand the board (32 × 7 in.) and paint or stain it. On a firm surface, place an old towel as padding to drill the holes in the cups. Determine the center for the holes and mark with masking tape on both sides.

Put on the protective gloves and safety glasses. Use the drill with a diamond-tip bit to drill into the pattern side of the saucer and the inside of the cup in the marked positions. Drill briefly, then put a little water in the dent you made, to prevent the drill from becoming too hot. Proceed in the same way for all cups and saucers.

2. Now decide the position on the board for the holes to attach the cups and saucers. If the cups have different-sized handles, it's important to position them so that the stick can be threaded through the handles on the same level. Use the wood drill bit to drill three holes for the cups and saucers and two further holes to hang up the board.

3. Now attach all coffee sets in this order: place a washer on the screw, then the cup, another washer, the saucer, and another washer. Then insert the protruding part of the screw through the hole in the board and secure with a nut. Insert the stick (approximately 32 in. long) through the handles and hang on the wall.

ALWAYS ON HAND. IT'S SO NICE WHEN EVERYTHING HAS ITS OWN PLACE IN THE KITCHEN AND WHEN THE UTENSILS CAN BE PRETTILY PRESENTED.

Pop Cup

MATERIALS:
WHITE MUGS, AN OLD PLASTIC CONTAINER, PAPER TO USE AS A DROP CLOTH, DISPOSABLE GLOVES, WOODEN STICKS, PAPER TOWEL, MARBLING PAINTS

EVEN OLD OR BORING COFFEE MUGS CAN BE EASILY TRANSFORMED. WITH THE MARBLING TECHNIQUE, IT'S CHILD'S PLAY TO CREATE A COOL EFFECT ON THE MUGS.

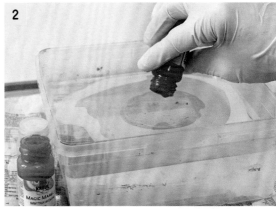

1. Cover your workspace with some old newspaper and collect your materials. Fill the plastic container with cold water.

2. Shake the paints well (I used neon pink, neon yellow, and neon orange). Put on disposable gloves and add the paint drop by drop to the surface of the water.

Start with the main color; in this example it is neon yellow. Then add the first decorative color; I used neon pink. Finally add some neon orange accents (see photo).

3. Use the sticks to mix the individual colors to create a marble pattern.

4. Now dip the mugs approximately 1.5 in. deep into the mixture. Holding the mug, slowly turn it so that the paint goes all around the mug (see photo). Pull out of the water.

Blow away any excess water or carefully wipe it off with a paper towel. After approximately eight hours, the plate should be completely dry. Some porcelain paints allow for oven drying; follow the manufacturer's instructions.

After you have marbled the plate, carefully soak up the excess paint from the used water with a paper towel before discarding the water.

The marbling paints used here are not food-safe or dishwasher-safe.

NEON LOVE. WHY NOT MAKE THE CANDLEHOLDERS A CENTERPIECE AND PLACE AN ASSORTMENT OF CANDLES IN THE MARBLED MUGS, HOLDING THEM IN PLACE WITH SOME FLORAL FOAM?

It's What's on the Inside That Counts

MATERIALS:
COFFEE CUP WITH A PATTERN ON THE INSIDE, SMALL PLASTIC BUCKET AS A MOLD, ENGRAVING DEVICE (E.G., DREMEL), CUTTING DISK SUITABLE FOR PORCELAIN, DISPOSABLE GLOVES, CEMENT MOLDING MATERIAL, OLD BOWL, KITCHEN SCALE, SANDPAPER, OIL, PAPER TOWEL

THIS LITTLE BOWL REALLY LOOKS LIKE AN EXPENSIVE DESIGNER OBJECT, YET IT'S SIMPLY A PERFECT EXAMPLE OF HOW TO RECYCLE A BROKEN CUP. CLEVERLY COVERED, IT CAN STILL BE ATTRACTIVE WITHOUT ITS HANDLE.

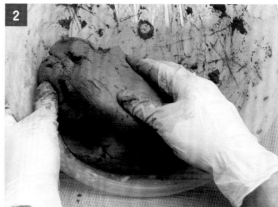

If the cup you are using still has a handle, then you should remove it first. Put on protective gloves and carefully use the cutting disk on the Dremel. If possible, leave approximately 1 cm of the handle so that the cup will not be damaged.

1. Now start work on the cement molding material. Wear protective gloves and safety glasses. Mix the cement and water in the bowl to the ratio stated on the packaging. For this bowl, you will need approximately 1.5 lbs. of concrete powder (however, the amount depends on the size of the mold).

2. Knead the mixture into a ball. It should roughly have the consistency of pie dough. Use the paper towel to oil the inside of the mold. It makes it easier to free the bowl later on.

3. Then place half of the cement molding material into the bowl and press the cup into it. Roll the rest of the cement into a sausage shape and press it around the sides of the cup. If your mold is transparent, you can see if and where you need to press the cement farther in. Fill the mold until the cement molding material reaches the top of the cup.

4. Depending on the manufacturer's instructions, allow it all to dry for approximately 24 hours. The cement should then be hardened, and the bowl can carefully be removed from the mold. The rim of the bowl can be smoothed out using medium-fine sandpaper.

Baby, It's Cold Outside

MATERIALS:
4 CUPS, SILVER ACRYLIC PAINT, A WIDE
BRUSH, LETTER STICKERS, 4 CANDLES, PINE
BRANCHES, CHRISTMAS DECORATIONS

IT DOESN'T ALWAYS HAVE TO BE VINTAGE CHINA; MODERN AND SIMPLE
PORCELAIN IS ALSO SUITABLE FOR UPCYCLING. A REALLY SIMPLE AND AFFORDABLE
ALTERNATIVE TO THE TRADITIONAL ADVENT WREATH ARE FOUR CANDLES STUCK
INTO PRETTILY DECORATED AND LABELED CUPS.

1. Start with the icicles on the cups. To make them, get a lot of paint on the brush and stroke the brush along the top of the cup so that the paint runs down the outside of it.

The icicles should be distributed so that there is enough space for the lettering.

2. After four to five hours, the drips should be dry, and you can stick on the letters according to the manufacturer's instructions. Then decorate according to your taste.

Candlelight Coffee

MATERIALS:
ESPRESSO CUPS, WAX BEADS, WAX DYE BLOCKS IN RED, BLUE, AND GREEN, CANDLE WICKS, EMPTY CAN, STRAWS, WOODEN STICKS

MAKING YOUR OWN CANDLES IS A SATISFYING CRAFT. IT'S NOT SURPRISING, BECAUSE THERE ARE NO CREATIVE LIMITS IN TERMS OF COLOR AND SHAPE. BY THE WAY, CHILDREN WITH ADULT SUPERVISION ALSO HAVE A GREAT TIME MAKING CANDLES.

1-2. Collect all your tools and place them on old newspaper next to the stove. Place a straw over each cup, center the wick in the cup, and secure it around the straw.

Now, in a small pan, bring some water to the boil. Fill the tin can with wax pellets and place it in the pan of boiling water. For one espresso cup you need approximately 6 teaspoons of wax pellets.

To achieve pastel colors, you only need a bit of dye. Simply cut a thin slice off a dye block and add to the wax pellets. Mix with a wooden stick.

3. Once the wax has liquified, pick up the tin using oven gloves, and carefully pour the content into the prepared espresso cup.

TIP
IF THE WAX COOLS TOO QUICKLY, A DEEP HOLE WILL FORM AROUND THE WICK. YOU CAN PREVENT THAT BY ALLOWING THE WAX TO COOL VERY SLOWLY. IT PAYS TO PLACE THE CANDLE IN A WARM PLACE OR TO CAREFULLY WRAP IT IN A TEA TOWEL.

Funky Christmas

REFILLING WORN-OUT COFFEE CUPS. WITH A CHEEKY COAT OF PAINT AND ALL KINDS OF CHRISTMAS DECORATION, THE CUPS BECOME THE HIGHLIGHT ON THE CHRISTMAS TREE. WRAPPED IN A CELLOPHANE BAG, THEY CAN ALSO BE A VERY PERSONAL GIFT.

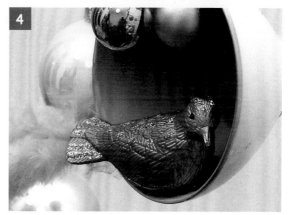

1. In particular, cups from the '50s are suitable for this project because they are funnel shaped with large openings. First choose the base color for the tree ornaments. It works best when you first paint the bottom of the cup and then paint from the inside outward up the sides. These cups often have a golden rim, and you should paint the inside up to this rim.

2. Snowman ornament:
Spray the inside of the cup with spray glue and then distribute the artificial snow. Use a decent amount of glue from the glue gun to stick the snowman in place. Attach gift ribbon to the handle.

3. Bauble ornament:
First carefully remove the hangers from the baubles. Then use a glue gun to completely cover the bottom of the cup and carefully press the small baubles into the glue. Allow the glue to dry and then glue in further baubles to taste. Attach gift ribbon to the handle.

4. Bird ornament:
Bird decorations are normally clipped to the tree branches. Carefully remove the clip. Then add a small dollop of glue on the edge of the cup, right below the handle. Now position the bird and allow the glue to dry. Tie three baubles together with gift ribbon and attach to the cup handle so that they hang into the cup. Stick a small pine branch over them and attach gift ribbon to the handle.

Lovely
Oddments

THE COFFEEPOT MISSING ITS LID, THE CUP WITHOUT THE SAUCER, THE LID FROM THE BROKEN SUGAR BOWL, THE CHIPPED CREAMER, OR THE EXTRA DESSERT PLATE. THE LIST GOES ON. THEY ARE ACTUALLY USELESS BUT OFTEN ASSOCIATED WITH HAPPY MEMORIES.

IF YOU LOOK AT THESE SOLOISTS A LITTLE MORE CLOSELY, YOU CAN SEE HOW MUCH ATTENTION TO DETAIL HAS GONE INTO THEIR DESIGN: THE COFFEEPOT USED TO BE THE QUEEN OF THE DECKED TABLE WITH HER ENTOURAGE OF MILK JUGS AND SUGAR BOWLS. REASON ENOUGH TO CREATIVELY RECYCLE THESE MAGNIFICENT PORCELAIN BIRDS OF PARADISE.

Dot, Dot, Dash...

MATERIALS:
SOUP OR SUGAR BOWL WITH 2 HAND-
LES, AN EGG CUP OR SIMILAR, SAUCERS,
GLUE GUN, BLACK PORCELAIN MARKER

WITH THEIR ROUNDED CHEEKS AND HANDLE EARS, SUGAR AND SOUP BOWLS CAN BE VERY CUTE. BUT WITH FACES DRAWN ON THEM THEY ARE SIMPLY MAGICAL.

1-2. The china should be clean and dry. It's best to test the porcelain marker on the bottom of the bowl to get a feeling for how it writes. First draw on the eyelid with short eyelashes. Then draw the line for the nose.

Stick the egg cup or saucer to the bowl with a small amount of glue from the glue gun.

Tips for decoration: To avoid waterlogging, place small pebbles in the soup bowl before using as a plant pot. Cut flowers are best displayed using floral foam.

Presented on a Plate

MATERIALS:
PLATTER OR SERVING PLATE, PORCELAIN
CUPBOARD KNOBS INCLUDING SCREWS AND
NUTS, RUBBER WASHERS, DRILL, DIAMOND-TIP
BIT, MASKING TAPE, PROTECTIVE GLOVES,
TILE NIPPERS, FLORAL WIRE

OVAL SERVING PLATES OR LONG DESSERT PLATES ARE WELL SUITED FOR
ATTACHING DECORATIVE PORCELAIN KNOBS. IT TURNS THEM INTO UNIQUE
JEWELRY HANGERS FOR NECKLACES AND BRACELETS.

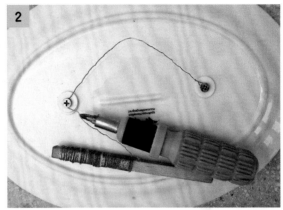

1. First decide on the position of the porcelain knobs. It's best to mark the position with masking tape on both sides of the plate. In this example, only two holes are drilled in the plate. To do this, find a firm surface and lightly pad with an old towel.

Put on the protective gloves and start drilling through the plate from the pattern side. Drill briefly, then put a little water in the dent you made, to prevent the drill from becoming too hot. Now drill the second hole.

2. Place a washer next to the hole on both sides of the plate, insert the porcelain knob through the washers and the hole, and carefully tighten the nut on the back. Now wrap the wire between the washers and the nuts on the back of the plate to form a hanger.

3. This pretty project is now finished, and you can present your favorite necklaces on a plate.

Swan Lake

MATERIALS:
PORCELAIN VASES AND JUGS; PORCELAIN
PAINT IN THE COLORS CHAMPAGNE, ROSE
GOLD, AND SILVER; BRUSHES

WOW, THE TREASURES YOU CAN FIND IN THE ATTIC! GIVE '60S STYLE SOUVENIR VASES A NEW COAT OF PAINT AND THEY BECOME STYLISH ORNAMENTS IN THE WINK OF AN EYE.

1. Clean the porcelain ornaments well, making sure that there is no dirt on the material. Apply the paint.

2. Allow the first coat of paint to dry for approximately four hours. If some patterns are still showing through, apply a second coat of paint.

TIP:
SMALL PIECES OF CHINA, WHICH ARE INTENDED ONLY TO BE ORNAMENTS, CAN ALSO BE PAINTED WITH NAIL POLISH. THEY MAKE PRETTY GIFTS FOR YOUR FRIENDS IF YOU USE THEIR FAVORITE COLOR.

Raise Your Cups

MATERIALS:
POTS, JUGS, EGG CUPS, SMALL BOWLS
AND SEVERAL SAUCERS, GLUE GUN

WORKING ON THESE CANDLEHOLDERS IS A LITTLE LIKE PLAYING WITH
CHILDREN'S BUILDING BLOCKS. AND JUST LIKE BACK IN THE PLAYROOM DAYS, IT'S
REALLY FUN WHEN YOU CAN MIX UP VARIED SHAPES.

1. The secret is in the mix. It's important that the pieces of china are level at the top so that the next saucer will have some support. For a stable candleholder, begin with a saucer at the bottom and then pile it up as you like.

2. Once you have found your favorite shape, it's time to deploy the glue gun. Make sure the china is clean and dry. Take the tower apart again and then stick it together, starting from the bottom. Spread the glue from the glue gun on both pieces and press them together. Allow to dry. Connect all pieces together in this way.

TIP:
THE TOWER SHOULD ALWAYS FINISH WITH A
PIECE THAT CAN BE USED AS A CANDLEHOLD-
ER. EGG CUPS OR CHINA FROM A DOLL'S TEA
SET CAN HOLD TYPICAL HOUSEHOLD CANDLES.
BOWLS OR SAUCERS ARE IDEAL FOR PILLAR
CANDLES.

Swinging Free

MATERIALS:
THREE SMALL BOWLS OR SOUP BOWLS, DRILL,
DIAMOND-TIP BIT, PROTECTIVE GLOVES,
MASKING TAPE, APPROXIMATELY 4 YARDS OF
CORD (MEDIUM STRENGTH), TAPE

CONTRASTS ATTRACT. IN THIS PROJECT, CHINA WITH DELICATE PATTERNS IS COMBINED WITH RUSTIC CORD. THE DRILLING IS NOT EASY, SO IT'S BEST TO HAVE A HELPING HAND.

1. Mark out where to drill the three holes on the lowest bowl. Then place the next bowl in the first one and mark where the holes should go so that they line up with the other holes. Repeat the procedure for the top soup bowl.

2. Now drill all nine holes. Find a firm surface and lightly pad with an old towel. It works best when somebody holds the bowl in place, so the side lies flat on the firm surface. Put on the protective gloves and start drilling the hole in the marked position from the pattern side. Drill briefly, then put a little water in the dent you made, to prevent the drill from becoming too hot.

When all the holes have been drilled, cut the cord into three equal lengths of approximately 1.3 yards.

3. Tie a secure knot at the bottom of the cord lengths. Wrap tape around the other end of the cord lengths to make it easier to thread it through the drilled holes. Now thread a cord through each hole in the bottom bowl.

4. About 4 in. up the cord lengths, tie another knot in each length and thread the second bowl onto the cord lengths. Repeat with the soup bowl. Tie the top ends of the cord together.

Pin Cushion

MATERIALS:
SUGAR BOWL WITH THE LARGEST POSSIBLE OPENING, FLORAL FOAM, COTTON, FABRIC SCRAP, YARN, GLUE GUN

SUGAR IS OUT AND UPCYCLING IS IN! THIS LITTLE BOWL WILL GIVE YOU A REAL SURPRISE. IT LOOKS AS SWEET AS SUGAR, AND AT THE SAME TIME IT'S REALLY PRACTICAL AND EASY TO MAKE.

1. Cut out a disk approximately 1 in. thick from the floral foam and press it into the lid. Use a knife to cut it into a round shape.

Cut out a circular piece of fabric. The diameter should be slightly bigger than that of the sugar bowl.

2. Place the cotton followed by the floral foam onto the wrong side of the fabric.

3. Pull the fabric together behind the floral foam and secure with the yarn. Cut off excess fabric. Use the glue gun to spread glue over the entire inside of the lid, and press the pin cushion into the lid.

Gifted with Love

MATERIALS:
HANDLES THAT HAVE BEEN BROKEN OFF CUPS (OR ORNAMENTAL CUPS WITH PRETTY HANDLES), TILE NIPPERS, PROTECTIVE GLOVES, GLUE GUN

THE BEAUTIFULLY DECORATED HANDLES OF TRADITIONAL 1950S ORNAMENTAL CUPS ARE TRUE GEMS. THEY ARE SOMEHOW REMINISCENT OF A HALF HEART, SO WHAT CAN BE MORE FITTING THAT TO MAKE TWO BROKEN HEARTS INTO ONE HAPPY HEART.

1. If you don't have any handles that have already broken off from cups, then you should carefully break the handle from a cup. Remember to wear protective gloves, because the small shards of china can be nasty.

To remove the handle, place the nippers on the cup next to the handle and snap.

2. Usually the whole handle comes away (see photo). Carefully break off excess porcelain.

3. Now cover the two handle ends on both handles with glue (see photo). For a heart hanger, you need two handles. They are glued together in the shape of a heart. Now use a glue gun to cover the two handle ends on both handles with glue, and press together.

Lovely Lids

MATERIALS:
PORCELAIN LIDS FROM COFFEEPOTS AND
SUGAR BOWLS, STURDY WIRE, CORK, WIRE
CUTTERS

Alles Gute!

WHAT ARE
YOU WAITING
FOR?

MARCH

MONDAY
1

£600 Frank

TUESDAY
2

WEDNESDAY
3

2021

THURSDAY
4

FRIDAY

SATURDAY
6

SUNDAY
7

IT'S ANNOYING WHEN YOUR FAVORITE COFFEEPOT BREAKS! YET, IT COULD BE A BLESSING IN DISGUISE IF THE LID REMAINS INTACT, MEANING YOU CAN USE IT FOR THIS CREATIVE PROJECT. IN THIS PROJECT, THE LITTLE LID IS MADE INTO A DECORATIVE HOLDER FOR PHOTOS, POSTCARDS, ETC.

1–2. First cut off approximately 6 in. of wire and wind it tightly around the knob on the lid several times.

Now wind the remaining wire around the cork. Once you have made a small spiral, remove the cork. In the spiral formed by the cork, you can stick postcards or notes.

Wall Light

MATERIALS:
LONG CAKE PLATE, EGG CUP, MASKING
TAPE, DRILL, DIAMOND-TIP BIT, PROTEC-
TIVE GLOVES, 4 WASHERS, SCREWS WITH
MATCHING NUTS, PLATE HANGER

PRETTILY COMBINED COLORS MAKE A BEAUTIFUL CANDLESTICK HOLDER OUT OF A CAKE PLATE AND EGG CUP. YOU CAN ALSO USE A ROUND PLATE AS THE BACK, OR SOMETHING ELSE ENTIRELY. THERE'S JUST SO MUCH CHOICE!

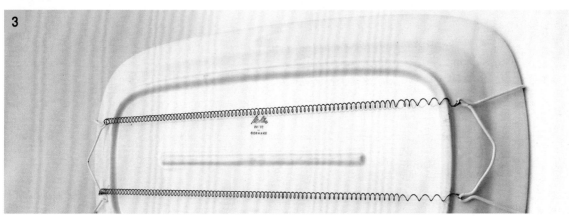

1. First drill the holes in the plate and in the egg cup. To do this, find a firm surface and lightly pad with an old towel. Now decide on the positions of the holes and mark with masking tape on both sides. The hole on the plate should be in the lower quarter so that there is enough space for the egg cup. Then mark the position on the side of the egg cup with masking tape.

Put on the protective gloves and start drilling in the marked positions. Drill briefly, then put a little water in the dent you made, to prevent the drill from becoming too hot.

2. Once you have drilled the holes, you can join the two pieces of china together. Add a washer on the inside and outside of the egg cup and behind the plate and thread the screw through them all. Finally, fix in place by screwing a nut on the back of the screw.

3. Attach a plate hanger on the back.

Get a Handle on It

MATERIALS:
WHITE CHINA (POT, CUP, ETC.), MASKING
TAPE, PORCELAIN PAINT, BRUSH

COFFEE COMES FROM THE COFFEE MACHINE THESE DAYS, DOESN'T IT? BUT WHAT ABOUT COFFEEPOTS? IT'S TOO MUCH OF A SHAME TO LEAVE THEM UNUSED. IF YOU GIVE THEM AN OPTICAL-REJUVENATION TREATMENT WITH A LICK OF PAINT, THEN IN NO TIME YOU HAVE A UNIQUE VASE. AND BECAUSE IT'S SO MUCH FUN, THE MATCHING LITTLE CUP ALSO GETS A PAINT JOB.

1-2. Painting is easier if you stick masking tape around the handle.

It's best to use just a little paint at first and then add a second coat.

BEAUTIFULLY SIMPLE. WHEN SPARINGLY USED,
NEON PAINT IS VERY MODERN.

Put the Plug in the Jug

MATERIALS:
2 SMALL BOWLS, 2 JUGS, DRILL, DIAMOND-
TIP BIT, MASKING TAPE, THREADED
ROD, SCREWS, WASHERS, TRANSPARENT
CORD, FLIP SWITCH, PLUG, HALOGEN BULB,
WIRE CUTTERS

THIS TABLE LAMP WILL BE VERY STABLE IF YOU USE A PIECE OF CHINA WITH
A DIAMETER THAT IS AS LARGE AS POSSIBLE, SUCH AS A SOUP BOWL OR SUGAR
BOWL, AS ITS BASE.

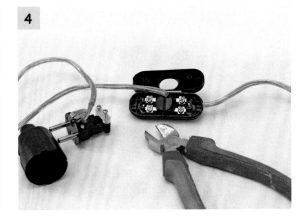

1. First drill the holes for the threaded rod (in this example, approximately 0.3 in.) and the cord. Mark with masking tape on the underside the center of the pieces of china. Put on the protective gloves and start to drill in the marked positions on the underside. Drill briefly, then put a little water in the dent you made, to prevent the drill from becoming too hot. Drill holes in all four pieces in this way.

2. Drill an additional hole for the cord in the side of the bowl.

3. It is important to work from top to bottom. Push the threaded rod (length is the same as the piled pieces) and the cord through the hole into the top jug and work downward. After each

piece of china, place a washer on the threaded rod and fix it in place with a nut.

Work in this way for all the pieces. The nuts should not be too tight since that could cause the china to break.

4. When all the porcelain has been joined together and the cord (in this example, approx. 0.75 in.) has been threaded through the side hole on the bowl, the electrics are assembled. (Length is the same as the piled pieces.)

The relevant poles have to be connected to each other. If you don't feel confident about doing this, you can buy preassembled cords with switches.

IT'S BEST WHEN THE BOWLS AND POTS ARE DIF-FERENT SIZES SO THAT THEY CAN BE PILED EASILY. IN THIS EXAMPLE, A LARGE POT AND BOWL HAVE BEEN COMBINED WITH A SMALL BOWL AND JUG.

Industrial Chic

MATERIALS:
CHINA BOWL, BRUSH, SPATULA, DISPOSABLE
GLOVES, CONCRETE PASTE, DROP CLOTH

SICK OF '70S STYLE? WITH THE HELP OF CONCRETE PASTE, AN OLD BOWL GETS A NEW, ULTRACOOL DESIGN IN NO TIME.

1. When using concrete paste on a smooth surface, such as porcelain, the surface should be covered first. Use a brush and the paste to paint the bowl on both sides.

2. When the pattern is no longer visible, you have the perfect base. Allow the paste to dry.

3. Now use the spatula to spread the paste generously with sweeping movements over the bowl, starting at the top rim.

4. To "concrete over" the base of the bowl, I used a silicon kitchen spatula. It's more flexible and creates softer joins. When finished, clean the spatula immediately with a paper towel. Depending on the thickness of the concrete layer, it can take 24 to 48 hours to dry.

Bed and Breakfast

MATERIALS:
COFFEEPOT, CUP AND SAUCER, THICK
WOODEN BOARD, DRILL, WOOD BIT,
DIAMOND-TIP BIT, PROTECTIVE GLOVES,
MASKING TAPE, 5 SCREWS, NUTS,
SCREWDRIVER, WASHER, PLIERS, WIRE

EVEN THE PRETTIEST COFFEEPOT IS USELESS WITHOUT ITS LID. BUT WITH ITS MATCHING COFFEE SET, THIS DISCARDED CHINA CAN BECOME A LOVELY NESTING AND FEEDING STATION FOR BIRDS.

1. Prepare the board however you choose. In this example, I sanded and oiled it. Alternatively, you can paint it to match the pottery.

2. Now decide on the position of the pot and cup. Mark the positions and drill the holes using the wood bit.

Prepare the china. You need a hole in the center of the jug base, a hole in the side of the saucer, and two holes in the cup: one in the center of the base and the other on the cup side exactly opposite the handle. Mark the positions on both sides with masking tape.

Now use the diamond-tip bit. Find a firm surface and lightly pad with an old towel. Put on the protective gloves and start drilling through the china from the pattern side. Drill briefly, then put a little water in the dent you made, to prevent the drill from becoming too hot.

First connect the saucer to the coffee cup. Stick a small screw through the side hole of the cup and into the hole in the saucer and tighten with a nut.

Continued on the following page.

Now attach the pot to the board. Place the pot over the predrilled hole and, using the pliers, push the screw through the hole inside the jug and the hole on the board. Tighten the screw with a screwdriver and fasten with a nut. When doing so, make sure the handle is pointing upward.

3. Attach the cup and saucer set to the board with a screw through the bottom of the cup. Fasten with a nut.

4. To hang up the board, screw two screws into the back and loop the wire around them to form a hanger.

THIS IS THE PLACE TO BE. LITTLE BIRDS WILL TELL EACH OTHER THAT A ROMANTIC BIRD HOTEL WITH NESTING BOX AND FEEDING STATION IS NEW IN TOWN.

Dinner Is Served

MATERIALS:
CHINA SERVICE CONSISTING OF A CUP, SAUCER, AND CAKE PLATE; CAKE STAND LEGS, WASHERS, ANTIRUST PAINT IN GOLD, BRUSH, DRILL WITH PORCELAIN BIT, PROTECTIVE GLOVES, MASKING TAPE, CORD

MIX AND MATCH. THIS FEEDING STATION IS MADE OF AN ASSORTMENT OF DISCARDED CHINA. OR YOU COULD USE A MATCHING SET.

1. So that the cake stand legs don't rust, give them a coat of antirust paint. To do this, stick the legs in floral foam, paint them, and then allow them to dry well.

In the meantime, drill the holes for the legs in the china. To do this, find a firm surface and lightly pad with an old towel. Now decide on the positions of the holes and mark with masking tape on both sides of the china.

Put on the protective gloves and start drilling through the china from the pattern side. Drill briefly, then put a little water in the dent you made, to prevent the drill from becoming too hot.

Drill holes in the cake plate, saucer, and cup in this way.

3. As soon as the cake stand legs have dried, you can screw the service together. Start by positioning a washer, the saucer, and the cup on a screw and screw the first leg on to it. Then place a washer on the leg and position the cake plate. Put another washer on top of the cake plate and attach the final leg.

Attach the cord to hang up the feeder.

About the Authors

Ina Mielkau is a visual merchandiser. She studied communication design and worked for over 15 years as a graphic artist. Although she loves her work on the computer, she also likes being in the craft studio and working with "real" tools. Ina is the author of 10 craft books on topics ranging from origami to concrete to eco-crafting. For many years she's been sharing her projects and design insights on her blog. She lives in Darmstadt, Germany. www.ynas-design.blogspot.de

Petra Knoblauch is a freelance stylist for international advertising campaigns in fashion, sports, and knitting. Her styling talents come in handy as she designs craft projects. A few years ago, she achieved her dream of having her own garden, and her favorite project was creating her garden stepping-stones from lovingly assembled shards of china. @petraknoblauch | www.petraknoblauch.com